# REBEL WITH A CAUSE:

## THE DOC NIKAIDO STORY

BRETTON LONEY

**FriesenPress**

Suite 300 - 990 Fort St
Victoria, BC, Canada, V8V 3K2
www.friesenpress.com

**ISBN**
978-1-4602-6914-5 (Hardcover)
978-1-4602-6915-2 (Paperback)
978-1-4602-6916-9 (eBook)

*1. Biography & Autobiography*

Distributed to the trade by The Ingram Book Company

# DEDICATION:

To my lovely and talented wife, Karen Shewbridge, who has supported this project, and all of my writing, from the very beginning. For my children Kier and Cale, their partners Kirk and Amy, and my grandson, Jonis.

To my mother, Jeanette Loney, who taught me the love of reading and writing, and to my late father, Roy Loney, who taught me the importance of hard work and perseverance—all crucial traits for a writer.

To the people of Bow Island, who helped raise so many children, including myself and my brothers Todd and Troy, by teaching us life lessons in their homes and classrooms, and on the hockey rinks and ball fields of our childhood.

# TABLE OF CONTENTS

Chapter 1—The Party...................................................1

Chapter 2—Doc The Character – First Impressions.............5

Chapter 3—A Visit To The Doctor's Office.......................9

Chapter 4—A Boy Named "Har".................................13

Chapter 5—The University Of Toronto Years....................20

Chapter 6—Bow Island...............................................28

Chapter 7—Doc Chooses Bow Island............................34

Chapter 8—Doc The Doctor – Going The Extra Mile..........39

Chapter 9—Doc The Doctor – The Innovator...................42

Chapter 10—Doc At Play...........................................44

Chapter 11—Doc The Doctor – The Master Diagnostician...49

Chapter 12—House Calls............................................52

Chapter 13—Doc The Doctor – Professional Detachment....56

Chapter 14—Doc Fights The Tax Man ............................. 58

Chapter 15—The Mentor ................................................ 64

Chapter 16—Road Trip ................................................... 67

Chapter 17—Doc's Personal Life ................................... 71

Chapter 18—A Night At The Hospital ........................... 74

Chapter 19—The Hospital Crisis Of 1969 ..................... 79

Chapter 20—Doc Runs For Town Council ...................... 84

Chapter 21—Doc's Death ............................................... 87

Chapter 22—The Funeral ............................................... 90

Epilogue ........................................................................ 93

Acknowledgements ........................................................ 97

Sources .......................................................................... 99

# CHAPTER 1
## The Party

*March 1, 1973*

Dr. Harry Nikaido squirms at the front of the packed hall, uncomfortable in the new dress pants, shirt, sweater, tie, and shoes that his friends bought him for this special night. He may be the only doctor in southern Alberta who does not own a suit, and he couldn't care less.

Tomorrow patients will see his familiar ball cap, baggy pants, and a lab coat, with the pockets of his rumpled sport shirt groaning with pens, and his sockless feet thrust into crumpled, laceless shoes.

The walls of the Legion are decorated with large reproductions of the notes Doc is famous for leaving on his office door:

At the hotel, be back at 4:00. Harry Nikaido

At the golf course, be back at 3:00. HN

If you don't let the phone ring at least 6 times, don't bother to call. HN

Cure for colds: Go to bed earlier. Drink plenty of fruit juices. Come back in a week. HN

Outside, the evening is cooling after an unusual winter's day that saw temperatures rise to 10 C and one brave crocus, in a nearby garden, stick its head out of the melting snow. Spring is near and people are in a good mood.

The audience settles in to listen to Dave Pickard, a retired school principal with thick frame glasses. He is one of many speakers at this Recognition Night to honour Doc for 22 years of service to the small, Alberta community of Bow Island.

"Dr. Nikaido has been present when new life was born and when death was in our midst," Dave says. "When we have needed him, he has been there."

Heads in the packed hall nod in agreement, Fred Mellen's among them.

Ten years earlier, Fred's wife went into labour two months early. The hospital called Doc and he drove through the night, from a wedding he was attending three hours away, to deliver the baby.

Clara Fraser, one of the evening's organizers, recalls Doc driving out to her farm house when her two young daughters were down with measles and suffering high fevers. He stayed until after midnight to be sure the girls were okay.

"Doc's benevolence and dedicated service have touched most, if not all of our families," says Dave. "His service to others and utter disregard for material gain, is something that many of us don't understand. It's the way Doc is, and we love him for it."

More heads nod. Before universal Medicare, Doc charged patients only a couple of bucks per visit, in cash. Sometimes patients never had to pay at all.

Bill Noviski, a long-time friend and patient, rises next. Doc's diagnosis saved his son's life when perplexed doctors in nearby Medicine Hat had given up hope for the one-year-old who was convulsing and turning blue. It is one of many stories told about the extraordinary care Doc provided over the years.

Soon it is time for presents for the man of honour. The crowd erupts in laughter as a man appears riding a new, 10-speed bike through the narrow aisles of the packed hall, a shiny medical bag strapped to the back. He is dressed to look like Doc, wearing a white doctor's coat and a John Deere baseball cap. Later in the evening, a nurse snaps a photograph of Doc riding the bike up and down the hallways of the hospital.

Farmer Herb Thacker presents a pair of curling shoes, but not before taking a good-natured jab at Doc who is a fierce competitor in many sports. He jokes that Doc is a better golfer in the winter and curls better in the summer. Herb goes on to commend the doctor for his selfless dedication in an era when everyone is after the almighty dollar.

The main gift of the evening is a portable colour television, so that Doc can watch his favourite sports: hockey, football, baseball and golf. Weeks earlier, the night's organizers had approached Doc about giving him a new car to replace his latest wreck, but he turned down the offer as too generous. Later, he donates the TV to the patients' lounge at the Bow Island Hospital, where he often crashes to watch it after a hard day.

He receives a photo album with pictures of the 163 babies he has delivered since coming to Bow Island, including eight siblings from one family. His second family, the nurses at the hospital, put the album together.

A birthday cake is wheeled out to celebrate Doc's recent 53rd birthday. His life's journey has taken him from his birth in Vancouver, in 1920, to Toronto in 1941, to earn his medical degree, to Regina to intern, and finally to Bow Island in 1951.

The arc of his life was dramatically altered by the forced resettlement of the Nikaido family from their home in Vancouver during World War II. The Nikaidos were among the 22,000 Japanese Canadians whose world was torn apart by an order-in-council passed by the federal Cabinet, under the War Measures Act, in 1942. It created a 100-mile protected strip along the Pacific coast, which all Japanese Canadians were forced to evacuate. The Nikaidos lost their house, business, and automobile.

This dark stain in Canadian history, during which Ottawa acted so unjustly against Japanese-Canadians in a way it never treated German or Italian-Canadians, is mentioned in passing by one of the night's speakers who hastily moves on to happier times and to celebrating Doc's life.

Doc gets up to speak. He begins nervously, apologizing for his lack of training as a public speaker, but goes on to deliver a touching and humorous speech that pokes fun at his many friends, colleagues, and patients in the room.

The night ends with music from two orchestras, including Doc's friend Bill Noviski, a trumpeter and local band leader. Doc doesn't dance. Instead he circulates through the crowd, shaking men's hands and kissing women.

He is pleased with how the evening is turning out. It is an affirmation of his adult life and a profound turn of events, given that four years earlier he was nearly drummed out of town in a controversy that saw one doctor lose his hospital privileges and leave.

As Doc soaks in the esteem of friends, an off-duty RCMP officer sits in the crowd with a warrant for Harry Nikaido's arrest in his pocket. The Mountie tells one of Doc's closest friends that he doesn't want to serve the warrant this evening as it might start a riot. He is right.

**Hospital colleagues Gail McNeely, Dixie Johnson, Mavis Weatherhead and Doris Campbell, surround Dr. Harry Nikaido at a special night held in his honour on March 1, 1973 to honour his 23 years of service to the community. Doc's friends bought him dress clothes for the evening so that he could look his best.**

# CHAPTER 2
## Doc The Character – First Impressions

The first time Alex Zhou met Harry Nikaido, the doctor was lying outside on the oil-stained ground underneath his beat-up car, up to his elbows in grease, making repairs. Alex and his pregnant wife, Judy, had just moved to Bow Island from Saskatchewan and were looking for a new physician. They had wandered outside after finding Doc's office on main street empty, with no receptionist to greet them.

"Is this guy a doctor?" Alex asked himself. "He looked more like a farmer that just came off the farm … he didn't look like a doctor."

Over the years, people have described Doc as looking like a blacksmith, a railway tramp, or a 1960s university professor, but never like a medical doctor. Certainly not the buttoned-down image of TV physicians of the 1950s and 60s like TV's Dr. Kildare or his real-life counterparts.

In 1959, young nurse Mavis (Gooding) Weatherhead had just moved to the newly opened Bow Island Hospital with her twin sister, Maureen, from Regina's Grey Nuns Hospital. Grey Nuns, an institution founded by the pioneering Sisters of Charity, was a spit and polish operation. Doctors wore suits, ties, and well-shined shoes and were addressed as "Doctor"— with a capital D.

Mavis met Dr. Nikaido walking the hallways in his bare feet, wearing an operating coat and no shirt. His paunch hung over baggy pants. He was known to use binder twine to keep them up when his belt was broken. A cigarette dangled from his lip. He needed a haircut and a shave. His thick

5

glasses were greasy. Even though he was only five feet, four inches tall, Mavis was intimidated.

Once she got to know him, she found Doc to be friendly and welcoming. He treated Mavis and the rest of the nurses with respect—as part of his team. Bow Island's two other doctors were friendly enough, but they were "Doctor Carr" and "Doctor Woolner". Kept on a pedestal. Harry Nikaido was simply "Doc".

Doc had no time for appearances or for the deference granted doctors. When he went out of town, he made a point of telling friends not to introduce him as a doctor to anyone they met.

Regardless of what people thought he did for a living, one thing was clear: Doc made an indelible first impression. People were floored by his appearance. Once they got to know him, they either loved him and were fiercely loyal or they were suspicious and cool to him; there was no in between.

Doc was an eccentric in a town crammed with individualists and mavericks. Like Frank Zorn, who ran a repair shop and could fix any TV or radio on the market. In the 1930s, he developed a homing device, the forerunner of radar. During World War II the air force dragooned him into civilian service to train their personnel on how to use the device and to teach radio communications.

Or like Jim Wutzke, who invented an automotive power source called the Vari-Power, which farmers could plug in to power electric tools in the field. The Vari-Power utilized the vehicle's engine battery to create electrical power, converting DC current to AC current.

Whether Doc was driving around in his hood-less Delta 88—the backseat piled high with clothing, car tools, sports equipment, and envelopes packed with pills—or sitting on a stool in the hotel bar engrossed in a newspaper, Doc was his own man.

Despite initial doubts, Alex and his family became Doc's patients and good friends. Alex ran the café in the hotel, down the block from Doc's office. Doc ate for free in exchange for providing free medical service in the days before Medicare.

"You keep me alive and I'll keep you alive," Doc always said to Alex when he popped in to eat, wandering through the kitchen to see what was cooking before he sat down at the counter. That could be any time of the day, as Doc didn't have a schedule like most people. He acted on impulse.

Doc had a voracious appetite. He could eat and eat and wasn't particularly fussy, although he loved a good steak and was partial to authentic Chinese food. He was well-known for the damage he inflicted, at a Medicine Hat restaurant, on its all-you-can eat smörgåsbord. If the opportunity arose, he would sit down to two or three Christmas dinners in a row. Afterward he might issue an earth-shaking belch, which he insisted showed appreciation for the meal.

Doc also had a real hunger for knowledge. He liked to know something about everything and always had his nose in a newspaper, book, or magazine—*TIME, Golf Digest, National Geographic,* or the latest medical journal.

No matter where he went, Doc contributed more than his share to the conversation with interesting, well-reasoned opinions. A friend described him as a Renaissance man who could talk intelligently on any number of topics. Another described him as a philosopher.

Listening to small talk bored him terribly. Sometimes he sat down and read the newspaper or watched TV in the midst of a party, if the conversation didn't interest him.

Doc was a heavy smoker, but like former U.S. president Bill Clinton, he didn't inhale as he didn't think it was good for you. Smoking was something he did socially. He didn't often buy cigarettes either, preferring to scrounge them, sometimes two or three at a time.

What he had no interest in was money or material things. He didn't own a house or cottage, bought only one new car during his 26-year medical career, and rarely took a vacation. He was the least materialistic person the town had ever seen. As long as Doc's belly was full and he had a roof over his head, whether that was crashing at a friend's place or sleeping sideways on three plastic chairs at the hospital, he was happy.

Doc also had a good sense of humour that could be clever and amusing as well as sometimes a bit silly. He crashed the Halloween party of his friend Bud Henningsgard's young teen-aged children, dressed in the painted face and bandages of a zombie. Doc and their older brother jumped through the window, accidentally breaking a pane of glass, and sent teens fleeing in every direction.

Another time he was about to give friend Merle Nelson a tonsillectomy. As Merle was being wheeled toward the operating room, Doc came around the corner sharpening two butcher knives, chortling with maniacal glee, before a nurse curtly told him to stop scaring Merle.

After Robin Dann's tonsillectomy, Doc suggested the teenager should run off and join a sideshow.

"With tonsils like that, you should be in the carnival," he said.

Doc brought to the practice of medicine a bright and inquisitive mind, a perfectionist streak, and a quiet compassion hidden underneath a rough exterior. One patient said that, when Doc listened to you describe your ailments and symptoms, it was like they became part of him. He knew exactly what he was going to do to fix your problem.

Doc's charitable nature did not extend to the Canadian government. He had a long-abiding hatred and mistrust of Ottawa because of its mistreatment of his family and other Japanese Canadians during World War II. How much the shame and indignity of Canada's draconian actions shaped and influenced Doc's life is an intriguing question, but one thing is certain: It was a betrayal Doc never forgot.

# CHAPTER 3
## A Visit To The Doctor's Office

A visit to Dr. Harry Nikaido was like a visit to no other doctor's office in Canada. It wasn't uncommon to find car tires and automobile batteries, a radiator, or even an engine in the corner of the waiting room. There were piles of paper everywhere. Newspapers, magazines, and books. Various personal items too, as it contained most of Doc's worldly possessions—at least the ones not stored in the back seat of his car. One person likened his office to the debris field from the Titanic, with flotsam and jetsam strewn across every square foot.

In the back was a storage room piled high with bottles of pills and free samples. Doc was one of the few physicians in Alberta also licensed as a pharmacist. He had no use for pharmacies and their high mark ups.

There wasn't usually a receptionist to greet patients and there were no standard office hours or appointments. Patients waited on a sagging chesterfield that sometimes doubled as Doc's bed. They might be there for a while, as no one knew when he would be in unless there was a hand-written sign on the door announcing that he was at the curling rink or golf course, and in theory, what time he might return. If Doc wasn't in, the sign on the door said something like: "When phoning me, if I am out of town, the hospital <u>always knows</u> how to reach me, otherwise I am either on the way to the hospital or at Myrtle Hotel Bar and Coffee Shop. Always call the hospital and leave a message or if urgent have <u>the hospital</u> phone me."

Sometimes he opened for business at 9 or 10 a.m., saw patients for a while and then took a break for lunch. Other times he saw patients all day without a break. Every once in a while, Doc snuck out the back door if he spied a patient out front that he didn't want to see. He had no time for hypochondriacs.

Doc's patient records were in no better shape than the rest of the office. There were no filing cabinets with carefully labelled files. No reams of alphabetically-ordered paper. Instead, patient files were stacks and stacks of paper piled three-feet high on a small table. Once the patient finally managed to get in, Doc asked for the date of his last visit. Then he paused for a second, searched for the right pile of papers among many, and presto, pulled out a sheet of paper with the patient's medical information. It was medical record magic and everyone marvelled at his sleight of hand.

As unconventional as his office was, Doc's approach to payment for services was more extraordinary. Money was never an issue. Prior to Medicare, Doc only charged patients one or two dollars per visit, in cash, never more. Sometimes patients walked in and out without paying a cent. Some people he charged immediately. Others he promised to catch later. Every once in a while Doc ran into Donald Jenkins, whose family were patients, and asked him for $20 or $30, which Donald forked over.

Hospital administrator, John Nicolet, brought one of his children to see Doc for an appointment in the 1970s and asked how much he should pay. Doc asked to see the inside of John's wallet, took a look, grabbed a bill, and said, "I'll take this one."

One time a patient came in to see Doc and said she was afraid she couldn't pay him. "Who asked you?" was Doc's gruff response.

Some of the local Hutterites—a religious, communal branch of German-speaking farmers similar to the Amish—paid Doc with produce rather than cash, while other townspeople bartered with him for various services.

While Doc preferred cash, sometimes he accepted cheques. Patients knew that Doc was unlikely to cash them. He didn't want a paper trail the Government could follow—especially Revenue Canada. Friends helping him move into a new office found a shoe box with $65,000 worth of stale-dated cheques packed inside.

Any medicine he dispensed cost a bit extra. Doc's charge for prescriptions was whatever money he needed at the moment, but usually wasn't much.

"He might charge you $10 or he might charge you $20 or he might charge you nothing," says patient and friend Ella Nelson

When Medicare was implemented in 1966, he rarely filed any claims. He continued to charge fees that were below the Alberta hourly minimum wage for his entire medical career. Doc had his reasons for charging what little he charged and they had to do with getting back at the Canadian government. He wouldn't hesitate to share those reasons if you got to know him.

Doc's bedside manner could be brusque. He could not tolerate those who couldn't bear a little pain. One teen-age boy saw him at the hospital after reopening stitches that another doctor had put in while removing a small growth from his knee. The teen had torn them open playing baseball. Doc made a point of redoing the three or four stitches without an anaesthetic.

"It'll serve you right for ripping this open," he muttered.

Frustrated patients, tired of waiting to get in to see Doc, sometimes tried to circumvent the system by asking for consultations when they ran into him at the bar or a party. He found a sure-fire cure to stop this approach. He barked at them to strip and get up on the nearest table for an examination. Or, if he gave them any advice, it was to "quit drinking, quit smoking, and sleep in separate beds." No one asked for an after-hours consultation twice.

Not that Doc didn't take his "office" and services on the road. One of his favourite haunts was the City Café in nearby Medicine Hat. It was a Chinese restaurant on North Railway Street and one of the first places Doc stopped in Alberta when he moved from Saskatchewan to Bow Island. It was long and narrow with plenty of booths and a friendly, easy-going atmosphere. The kind of place that waitresses worked at for decades, becoming as familiar to regulars as the menu.

As always with Doc, the line between his personal and professional life was blurred if not utterly invisible. The City Café often doubled as his Medicine Hat office and he saw patients at a booth or in a room in the back. He let Medicine Hat patients know what time he would arrive, doing diagnoses on the spot and providing prescriptions and free samples. Sometimes the patients he saw at the café were from as far away as Calgary.

Even though Doc never had much money, the meal was often on him when he was at the café with friends. He was in tight with the owners, Ben Kong Yee and Tong Gong Yee in the early days, and later Willi and Cecil Wong. If the kitchen wasn't cooking up something special for Doc, besides its usual fare and "western style" Chinese food, he had a huge steak in front of him that covered his plate.

Over his 24 years in Bow Island, Doc had two different offices on the main street, another one in a small stucco house on the highway that bisects Bow Island, and finally an office in a white bungalow nestled among the double-wide trailers in the town's only trailer park.

Gradually Bow Island divided into two camps when it came to doctoring. In one were Doc's patients, including many farm families—people comfortable with his informal way of practising medicine and those who had challenges paying for medical care.

In the other camp were people who, if they had a choice, went to the other half dozen physicians who passed through town from 1951 to 1975. Some of them simply couldn't stomach Doc's dishevelled appearance and unorthodox practice without schedules, typed patient files, fee schedules, or order of any kind. Others discriminated against the "Japanese" doctor.

"Some people liked him and some people didn't," says Mavis Weatherhead. "There were quite a few people who treated him quite badly and talked about him badly."

Linda Volk, a former patient, agrees.

"He was shunned by a lot of people. There were people in town that went to Doc Nikaido and then there were people in town who went to other doctors. There were two whole sets of people and the people who went to Doc Nikaido loved him to death."

# CHAPTER 4
## A Boy Named "Har"

Harry Nikaido was rambunctious and headstrong from the day he was born, kicking and screaming, on February 29, 1920, in Vancouver, to Yoshi and Kimi Nikaido, and was the couple's third son and third of four children.

Yoshi and Kimi were first-generation Canadians. A teacher had encouraged Yoshi, a second son, to leave Japan's Fukushima Prefecture and the family farm and orchards in Toriwata to seek his fortune in the West. He tried Hawaii first, but left because the beautiful islands and wonderful weather "sap a man's ambition." He moved to California and worked his way up the west coast to Vancouver just before the First World War. He took a job as a chauffeur, complete with cap, knee-high boots, and a uniform with shiny buttons.

Yoshi went back to Japan in 1914, and after an arranged marriage, returned to Vancouver with his 19-year-old bride, Kimi (Yabuuchi). In later years, Yoshi joked that the Yabuuchi family tricked him. He told his children that he thought he was getting "the youngest, prettiest daughter and instead got the flat-nosed one who couldn't cook."

Kimi's family were well-to-do merchants and tradesmen. Her father was a watchmaker, who owned one of the first bicycles in their district. He liked to ride past astonished onlookers wearing a pith helmet, scaring local children who thought he looked like the devil riding down the country roads.

Yoshi was a quiet and gentle man, with glasses and a neatly trimmed moustache, who rarely complained. His bride, Kimi, was outgoing and friendly and always smiling. A tiny woman, she was a clothes horse who loved to wear high heels.

Kimi, who grew up in a household that had maids, found her first employment in Canada as a maid. The young couple quickly established their own dry-cleaning and dress-making shop on the 400-block of Robson Street, living above the business with their growing family. They attended a nearby United Church in the working-class neighbourhood.

Harry was the youngest boy, behind the oldest, Sadao, and Frank. A younger sister, Geri, completed the family. While Harry was his real name, his family called him Harley, or Har for short as his mother had a hard time pronouncing the letter "R", like many Japanese speakers.

Yoshi left the upbringing of the children to Kimi and they proved to be a handful—especially Har. Little sister Geri remembers Har getting a "tremendous walloping" one time after being bad and having a "ho-hum" look on his face afterward. The spanking had no effect.

The Nikaido home was 20 minutes away, by streetcar, from Japantown or Little Tokyo, the Vancouver Downtown East-side neighbourhood surrounding Powell Street and parts of Alexander Street. It was the economically vibrant epicentre of Japanese culture in Canada prior to 1941, as 95 per cent of the 24,000 people of Japanese descent in Canada lived in British Columbia. The first Japanese people settled in the neighbourhood in the 1890s, due its proximity to the Hastings Mill and jobs.

Japantown, or *Nihonmachi*, was the home of the Japanese Language School, the Buddhist Church, and the Japanese Hall. It also had hundreds of Japanese-Canadian-owned stores and businesses, ranging from restaurants, fish markets, and confectioneries (which sold imported sweets, such as manju) to Japanese-style public bath houses, newspapers, and banks. Reigning over the area's commercial life was Maikawa Department Store, the Japantown equivalent of Eaton's.

Little girls in homemade dresses skipped rope on the sidewalks as young boys pushed past on their scooters. Everyone dressed neatly and fashionably in Canadian clothing. Traditional Japanese clothing was only worn on special occasions, such as parades where women wore their finest kimonos and walked streets festooned with Japanese flags and Union Jacks.

Japantown also boasted Oppenheimer Park, where the popular all-Japanese Canadian baseball team, the Asahi (or Rising Sun), dominated the diamond over their cross-town Caucasian rivals. The Asahi's faithful fans willingly forked over 10 cents for a ticket to watch their heroes.

Back on Robson Street, the only other Japanese-Canadian families owned the grocery store across the street and a nearby confectionery. The Nikaidos spoke only English in their home. Yoshi was committed to learning the language of his adopted country and took English lessons throughout his life.

Har's older brother Sadao, who was sent to live with paternal relatives until his teens (like many eldest sons of the time), spoke fluent Japanese. Besides public school, the Nikaidos also sent Har and his brother Frank to Japanese School, where grammar, reading, calligraphy, and Japanese history were taught, but they played hooky and learned nothing. Still, they were promoted year after year so that the family wouldn't lose face.

When Har was nine years old, he visited Japan with his mother. One day, Kimi took him to Tokyo to a large department store where he promptly went missing. The adults frantically searched the store from top to bottom without success and headed back to their bed and breakfast to call the police, only to find Har already there, munching on an apple.

Somehow the Vancouver 4th grader, who didn't speak Japanese, had managed to find his way back through the bustling streets of Tokyo. Har said that he thought his mother told him to "go home." More likely, Kimi told him that they would go home if he didn't start behaving.

Har and Frank, who shared a bedroom and were two years apart, were inseparable, living a boyhood right out of a Little Rascals movie, full of pranks and adventures. Their playmates and classmates were English, Scottish, Hungarian, and Irish immigrants. One of Har's closest friends had flaming red hair and his mother, Madame Red, was a fortune teller.

One afternoon, as Geri came home by streetcar and passed over False Creek, she looked down and saw, to her horror, two black-haired boys and one red-headed boy skinny dipping in the water. It was her incorrigible brothers Har and Frank, with Madame Red's son. Later in life, Doc told friends about tobogganing as a kid on a cardboard box, sliding between the legs of a workhorse pulling a cart, and coming out the other side without a scratch.

A dangerous game that Har, Frank, and their buddies liked to play was to run along the packed logs floating and bobbing in Burrard Inlet, bound for one sawmill or another. The pastime cost the life of a young playmate who slipped underneath and drowned.

A free afternoon at the movies was also a boyish prank. The scam worked like this. One of Har's friends would buy a ticket for the ornate Orpheum Theatre on Smithe Street and head upstairs to the bathroom, where he would open a window. The rest of the gang shinnied up a nearby drainpipe and climbed through the window to free entertainment.

Another pastime was catching pigeons and selling them in Chinatown for 25 cents apiece. Har and Frank took turns swinging on a rope from a street light to the second-storey ledge of a building to grab the roosting birds.

Family dynamics always pitted Har and Frank against Geri and their older brother Sadao, whom they teased for his poor English. Forks and spoons sometimes whizzed through the air when sibling fights got too rowdy.

While Har wasn't a good student at Japanese school, he was a good, if wilful, student at Central Public School and later King George High School. Principal Gurley at Central Public called in Kimi for a chat about her son, whom he described as "pretty bright but in need of constant handling." Har was sent to the principal's office often enough at Central Public that Frank and Geri rarely had to buy school supplies. Har made good use of his time waiting in the office and stuffed his pockets with any nearby pencils and erasers.

The Nikaidos faced little overt racism in the Robson Street area among their Caucasian neighbours and friends, but racism and discrimination always existed in Vancouver for Asian Canadians, even for *Nisei*— Canadian-born children of Japanese, such as Har, his brothers and sister.

Since 1877, thousands of Japanese had immigrated to Canada to look for a better life (the first being a 19-year-old boy named Manzo Nagano, who jumped ship in Westminister, B.C). From the beginning, they faced discrimination. In the late 1880s, workers of Japanese origin were banned from joining unions, from working on Crown land in the forestry, and from better-paying jobs on the railroad. In 1895, B.C. denied the vote to all citizens of Asian origin. Due to this restriction, Japanese-Canadians couldn't become lawyers, pharmacists, architects, or chartered accountants as those positions were only open to those registered on the provincial voter's list.

In 1907, a mob of 8,000 people—whipped up by the anti-Asian immigration "Asiatic Exclusion League"—attacked Vancouver's Japantown and Chinatown, damaging 60 Japanese-Canadian businesses. In protest, Vancouver's Asian community went on a general strike for several days. Authorities roped off Japantown and Chinatown and held the communities under martial law for 10 days.

This backdrop of racism must have influenced Yoshi, who was a strong believer in higher education. He wanted his children to be well educated so that they could compete successfully with other Canadians for jobs, given that Japanese Canadians usually had to have more education than their European Canadian counterparts to be hired.

In the late 1930s, Japanese-Canadian university graduates faced nearly insurmountable hurdles finding employment in the few fields open to them, due to social taboos that discouraged Caucasian businessmen from hiring them.

From an early age, Har showed his lifelong passion for reading. As a youngster, he was a big fan of adventures series like the Bobbsey Twins and the Hardy Boys. Horatio Alger's rags to riches stories were a big draw too. Superman and Flash Gordon were favourite comic books. Later, he took breaks from reading books to pore through Popular Mechanics and sports magazines.

Armed with his Vancouver Public Library card, Har taught himself how to write shorthand, type, and speed read. He badgered Geri to take on the classics too, bringing home William Makepeace Thackeray's *Vanity Fair* for her to read, at age 12, and Fyodor Dostoyevsky's *The Brothers Kamarazov* when she was 15.

Har was not only a bookworm. He and Frank played lacrosse, often coming home with bloodied mouths—much to their mother's dismay. Har played a mean game of soccer, some rugby, and as he reached his early 20s, got frequent mention in *The New Canadian*, a local Japanese-Canadian English language newspaper, as a "hoopla wizard" and "sharpshooter" on the basketball floor. One game, he netted half the points his Maikawa's Hoopers' team scored.

He was a good enough student to move on to the University of British Columbia in 1937, where he was active on various sports teams, including the junior varsity soccer team, where he played half-back and was a team-mate of Yoshio Hyodo. The two were good buddies who shared a passion for sports, although both were only decent soccer players. Yoshio remembers Harry, as he was called in college, as being a bad dresser and not particularly social, earning the nickname "Gruff" among acquaintances.

"He wasn't a really outgoing or social person, but when you got to know him, it was an entirely different matter," says Yoshio.

One summer between university semesters, Yoshio and Harry worked on a small fruit farm in Mission B.C., 60 kilometres west of Vancouver on the Fraser River, picking strawberries, raspberries, blackberries, and blueberries. The farm's owners, the Nakashimas, were part of the size-able Japanese-Canadian community living in Mission prior to World War II, mostly involved in the berry industry, logging, and milling, as well as the inland fishery.

The Nakashimas employed Japanese-Canadian workers and European Canadians. The European Canadians lived in a bunkhouse, while the Japanese-Canadians lived downstairs in the Nakashima family home and shared traditional meals with the family.

"Harry didn't associate with the Japanese Canadians," says Yoshio. "He wanted to be with the Canadian fellows … he felt more at home with them."

Yoshio says Harry spent the summer living in the bunkhouse with the itinerant workers, eating baked beans, canned salmon, and custard.

More than 25 years later, one of the only overt acts of racism Har recalled to another friend, aside from the forced "evacuation" of Japanese Canadians from the coast in 1942, was an incident at UBC. He was convinced he was intentionally misled about what time a team photo was to be taken, to ensure the "Japanese guy" wouldn't be in the picture.

On May 14, 1941, *The New Canadian* celebrated Har as one of ten Nisei among 400 students graduating from UBC, a post-secondary institution that, at that time, had fewer than 40 Japanese-Canadian alumni. He received a Bachelor of Arts and was on his way to the University of Toronto where he would study medicine. Yoshio says it was a "big surprise" when he found out that Harry was accepted into medical school.

Harry was armed with good marks on his admission application to U of T, from a 90 in Chemistry and an 89 in Ancient History to 80s in English Composition, English Literature, and Physics. A 67 in Algebra was his weakest mark.

Har left Vancouver and his family behind in the summer of 1941, eagerly awaiting a fall he thought would be life changing. He was right in more ways than he ever could have imagined.

**In 1929 the 9-year-old Harry, far right in the bottom row wearing a cap and sweater, visited Japan with his mother, Kimi Nikaido, seated in the centre of the front row. Harry got lost while visiting a Tokyo department store but somehow the Vancouver 4th grader, who didn't speak Japanese, managed to find his way back to where the family was staying.**

# CHAPTER 5
## The University Of Toronto Years

Harry Nikaido arrived in Toronto in September of 1941, three months before the bombing of Pearl Harbour, eager for the academic challenges of medical school. He had two cousins in Toronto and moved in with them to live and work at the Alexandra Palace, a seven-storey hotel/apartment. Located in the Kensington-Chinatown neighbourhood near University Avenue, it was one of the city's first apartment buildings. It was demolished in 1968 to make way for the construction of Mount Sinai Hospital.

The University of Toronto Harry arrived at in 1941 was far different from campus today. There were few students of colour and fewer still in medical school. Anglo-Saxon names predominated—Brown, Stewart, Wilson, Pearson, and Fraser, with the occasional Goldberg. Men far outnumbered women, especially in graduate and professional schools like the Medical School, where less than 10 per cent of the students were women.

The rigours of medicine forced the athletic Harry to give up sports his first academic year at University of Toronto. He quickly befriended two freshmen, Bill Fielding and John Toogood, and took them under his wing, helping them adjust to the tough academic challenges. Soon Harry and his family faced far greater difficulties.

On December 7, 1941, the trajectory of Harry Nikaido's life and of his family thousands of miles away in Vancouver was forever altered by Japan's bombing of the American Pacific fleet at Pearl Harbour, Hawaii.

The surprise attack by 353 Japanese aircraft damaged or sank eight battleships, three destroyers, and three cruisers, and destroyed 188 fighter aircraft and killed 2,403 Americans, wounding 1,178 others.

It shocked the American people and directly led to America's entry into World War II, in the Pacific and in Europe, more than two years after Canada had declared war on Germany. The next day, U.S. President Franklin Delano Roosevelt described the attack as a "day that will live in infamy forever." It would have a lasting impact on Harry Nikaido.

No one knows how Harry heard the news or his reaction, but sister, Geri, then a 19-year-old student at University of British Columbia, will never forget.

"My brother Frank and I were sitting on the kitchen floor listening to the radio and wondering what was going to happen next. Of course we had no clue what was coming and how it was going to affect us."

Suspicion of Japanese nationals in Canada, and those of Japanese descent, was instantaneous, with wild talk of an imminent Japanese invasion in British Columbia. The screws immediately tightened on Japanese Canadians, nearly two-thirds of whom were Canadian born. At dawn on December 8, 1941, the Royal Canadian Navy started to impound the 1,200 vessels in British Columbia's Japanese-Canadian fishing fleet. Authorities shut down Vancouver's Japanese language schools as well as three Japanese-language newspapers. They allowed only *The New Canadian* English-language newspaper to continue publishing, but under heavy censorship.

Less than a week after Pearl Harbour, the Canadian Pacific Railway began letting go Japanese-Canadian section hands and porters. Vancouver's major hotels and sawmills quickly followed their example.

"Those days were so full of uncertainty and rumours," recalls Geri.

The focus was on coastal British Columbia, where the vast majority of Japanese-Canadians lived. On February 2, 1942 authorities proclaimed a night curfew "for all persons of Japanese racial origin in the protected area of B.C." Japantown came to a standstill at night, with no late ball games, judo practices, or other social activities. Far worse was to come.

Many of B.C.'s federal, provincial, and municipal politicians urged Prime Minister William Lyon Mackenzie King to take more drastic action. On February 16, 1942, Vancouver City Council unanimously passed a motion, by known anti-Asian politician, Alderman Halford Wilson, that called for the "removal of the enemy alien population from the Pacific coast to central Canada."

On February 24, 1942, the federal Cabinet passed an order-in-council under the War Measures Act giving authorities the power to intern "all persons of Japanese racial origin." It forced Japanese Canadians to evacuate the British Columbia coast, leaving behind homes, businesses, fishing boats, and vehicles, which were seized by the federal government.

Ottawa's action was not based on any real threat to national security. Canada's top military and police officers, as well as senior members of the civil service, strongly opposed the decision. The military refused to take part in the forced evacuation, arguing that it could not spare the manpower.

Two days later, the mass evacuation of Japanese-Canadians began. Some families received only 24 hours notice. Authorities sent men and boys to road camps. The elderly, women, and children were placed in internment camps in the interior of British Columbia. Some families were sent to work on sugar beet farms in Alberta and Manitoba, while others moved to Eastern Canada. Everyone could only take with them what they were able to carry. Adults were restricted to 150 pounds of belongings each and children to 75 pounds.

The federal government led them to believe that their possessions, properties, and businesses would be held in trust, but in 1943 they were liquidated. They lost everything, including bank deposits, stocks, and bonds.

In Vancouver, the Nikaidos were among the 22,000 Japanese-Canadians who saw their lives torn apart. Yoshi and Kimi were confused by what was happening to them in their adopted homeland. Their children, born and raised in Canada, were deeply hurt and angry. The Nikaidos lost their home, business, and the family car, which Yoshi had lovingly taken apart, greased, and put back together every Sunday. In 1942, Geri and Frank were among 76 Japanese-Canadian students kicked out of UBC, a small campus of about 2,500 undergraduates at the time.

"I was devastated," says Geri. "I didn't think my country, which is a democracy, could do this to me and others."

The family was being split up. Frank was sent to work at a lumber camp in Ontario, north of Lake Superior, while Sadao was ordered to work on a farm in southern Ontario. Father Yoshi was scheduled to go to a lumber camp in the interior of B.C..

Harry helplessly learned about the destruction of his family's life and the Vancouver Japanese-Canadian community from two thousand miles away. Letters to Harry from his mother and Geri sent him into a mixture of frustrated rage and deep depression.

Thirty-three years later, Dr. J.H. (John) Toogood will say that Harry Nikaido's "tough persistence under an appalling combination of social and academic pressures" that year "was probably more educational than any part of that long-forgotten curriculum."

Before authorities assigned Yoshi to a B.C. lumber camp, he offered to pay for himself, his wife, and daughter to move to Toronto, so that he could bring his family together in Ontario. Yoshi received some support for his case from John Toogood's father, a Toronto lawyer. The authorities agreed.

Yoshi carefully sorted the family's belongings, separating out what little they could bring to Toronto from what must be left behind, and packed them in a traditional, large Japanese straw basket. In the haste of their departure, he mistakenly brought a basket full of junk instead of the one with the family's clothing and shoes.

The Nikaidos arrived in Toronto in April 1942, and got off before Union Station in order to avoid a scene. They found a flat in a two-storey building at 160 McCaul Street in a predominantly Jewish neighbourhood near Queen's Park. Harry was happy to have his family safe nearby, but remained at the Alexander Palace with his cousins. Sometimes he would pop by the Nikaido's flat, with classmates John and Bill in tow, for all-night study sessions.

That same month, Vancouver Centre MP Ian Mackenzie, the federal Minister of Pensions and Health, returned to Vancouver to accept the praise of British Columbians for his role in the forced evacuation.

"It is my intention, as long as I remain in public life, to see they never come back here," Mackenzie told his constituents.

By November, 1942, 12,000 uprooted Japanese Canadians lived in the shacks and tenements of detention camps and ghost towns of the B.C. Interior, while 4,000 tried to stay warm in granaries and chicken coops across the prairies, where they had been sent to serve as farm labour. About 1,500 moved to Ontario and another 4,500 were in various locations in Canada outside the evacuation zone.

The war years in Toronto were difficult for the Nikaidos, as the prejudice stoked by the war grew. The local Japanese-Canadian community was small and could offer limited support. It was so tiny that some of the first families to arrive would go down to the Union Street train station each Sunday to see who else had come from B.C..

Geri began taking classes at Victoria College, on the University of Toronto campus, after U of T itself refused to admit her. Only the forceful intervention of a Victoria College professor shamed the U of T administration into relenting and allowing her to take courses at Vic and other university colleges.

Years later, Harry admitted to friends that he sometimes passed himself off during those years as Chinese, with the family name Lee.

Slowly Harry's life on campus became more normal. He immersed himself in his studies and renewed his passion for sports. He was an all-round athlete and at one time or another, in his six years at U of T, played intramural basketball, volleyball, water polo, rugby, and indoor baseball. He excelled at soccer and box lacrosse, in which he led the Medical School team to a Dafoe Cup victory.

In a 1944 story in the university's student newspaper, *The Varsity*, headlined "Varsity Lacrosse Whiz is All-Round Athlete", reporter Betty-June McKenzie described Harry as "five foot three inches of dynamite, weighing approximately 140 pounds."

"He is now known as the University's top ranking box lacrosse player … and has one of the most outstanding athletic records in the University," McKenzie wrote.

She went on to quote Harry's friend, "Mouse" Fielding, who said Harry is "the only man who can score a goal with five schoolmen on his neck." McKenzie described Harry as playing a "brilliant" game of basketball and a good game of water polo, volleyball, and soccer. Dick Shiozaki, Harry's future brother-in-law, met Harry late in his career at U of T, but his athletic reputation preceded him.

"I knew of his great reputation as a soccer player. Everyone on campus knew him as a great soccer player—rough and tumble."

On the surface, the gruff and tough Harry Nikaido remained, but the war, the evacuation, and the heightened racial discrimination left an indelible mark on the outwardly self-confident man. Before 1941, Harry saw a Canadian or a Canadian of Japanese descent when he looked in the mirror. The federal government would spend the 1940s convincing Canadians that the man Harry saw in that reflection was actually Japanese, not Canadian, and a potential enemy among us.

After the war, Harry never felt fully accepted in society among people he didn't know.

"I think the relocation and the racial discrimination that followed gave the doctor a very severe inferiority complex and he felt more at home among the lower classes of people," says friend Margaret Anderson.

In 1947, two years after the end of World War II and only one year after the forced evacuation to Japan of nearly 4,000 Japanese Canadians and a few Japanese nationals, Dr. Harry Nikaido graduated from the University of Toronto Medical School.

While Harry's graduation was not celebrated in the Toronto newspapers, *The New Canadian,* back home in Vancouver, proudly noted that of nine Nisei graduating from U of T, Harry was the only one graduating in medicine. It also pointed out that he was a "well-known Nisei athlete" and member of the senior soccer championship squad.

Harry headed west in 1947 to intern at Regina's renowned Grey Nuns Hospital, now called Pasqua Hospital. It was a prairie institution founded by the Reverend Sister Mary Duffin and the Sisters of Charity, who set out from St. Boniface, Manitoba in 1907 to bring medicine to the Saskatchewan pioneers. The hospital had a school of nursing, a cancer clinic, hundreds of patient beds, and the provincial laboratories.

No one knows why he chose Grey Nuns, or if there was much choice available to a Japanese-Canadian medical graduate in 1947. Some friends suggest he couldn't find an Ontario hospital where he could intern because of racism.

Returning home to Vancouver was out of the question. It was not until 1949, four years after the end of the war, that authorities removed the last wartime restrictions and allowed Japanese-Canadians to return to British Columbia.

Dr. Harry Nikaido interned in Regina for a couple of years, followed by a couple of years of practising medicine briefly in a number of small Saskatchewan towns, including Elrose, Biggar, Lipton, Grenfell, Mossbank, and Rockglen, before deciding to head farther west to Alberta.

**Harry Nikaido, bottom row far left, was a standout on the 1943 University of Toronto medical school senior lacrosse team and led the team to a Dafoe Cup victory. He also played intramural soccer, basketball, volleyball, water polo and rugby during his time at U of T. (Photo courtesy of University of Toronto)**

Harry Nikaido, bottom row far right, was regarded as
a fierce soccer player in his days at the University of
Toronto. He is pictured here with the 1944 medical school
soccer team which won the interfaculty championship.
Harry also played soccer for the University of British
Columbia's junior varsity soccer team before moving to
U of T. (Photo courtesy of the University of Toronto)

# CHAPTER 6
## Bow Island

In the beginning there were the heavens and the earth, but nothing much else where Bow Island presently stands. Perhaps a herd of passing buffalo, a pronghorn antelope, a coyote, or a preening grouse. The community sits on a vast sweep of prairies that stretches for hundreds of kilometres from the Saskatchewan border to the foothills in the shadow of the Rocky Mountains.

In its natural state, southern Alberta is dry, treeless, and flat. An unending vista of short grass, occasionally broken by deep coulees, which snake through the landscape in eye-catching relief to the flatland. Coulees are dry river valleys, created as the glaciers of the last ice age retreated into the welcoming embrace of the cold Rockies. It's as though God, in an impetuous moment, scooped out a piece of prairie and flung it out of sight.

Southern Alberta is the hottest part of the prairie provinces, with nearly 60 days per year when the thermometer reaches 26 Celsius degree or more and many days well into the 30s—a dry, searing heat like sitting too close to the fireplace.

It gets less than 38 centimetres of precipitation annually and one quarter of that is snow. One local used to say that in the Old Testament story of Noah, when it rained for 40 days and 40 nights, Bow Island only got half an inch. Some parts of the Bow Island area are so dry that prickly pear cactus and scorpions can be found. The nearest water is the South Saskatchewan River, ten kilometres northwest, which can get so shallow in high summer that you can walk across it.

Howling winds can blow at 100 kilometres per hour for days and gust as high as 170 kms, driving clouds of dust and grit across the countryside with the sting of buckshot. In the dead of winter, a warm Chinook wind from the west or southwest can melt the frigid landscape and spike temperatures by as much 20 to 25 degrees above zero centigrade in a matter of hours.

Before the arrival of white explorers in 1754, the region was home to the Blackfoot Confederacy or Nittsitapi First Nation, which in English means "original people". A small, natural spring three kilometres northwest of Bow Island was one of their watering stops. These nomadic hunters were always in search of the buffalo that streamed across the Prairies in rivers of flesh. Not only was the buffalo their primary food but its skin became teepees, and its hides, robes. The Blackfoot used buffalo fat to make soap and fashioned bones into tools.

The arrival of fur traders, followed soon by the white men who hunted buffalo for sport as well as their shaggy hides, and American whiskey traders, eventually led to the slaughter of the buffalo herds. It forever changed the Blackfoot and destroyed their nomadic hunter culture.

The Government of Canada purchased the region from the Hudson's Bay Company in 1870. In order to open the land to settlement, Ottawa negotiated treaties with various First Nations, including the Blackfoot, who in 1887 signed Treaty Number 7 and settled on reserves throughout southern Alberta. At the time, Calgary had fewer than 300 residents.

Before signing the treaty, Ottawa acted to bring law and order to the west and to southern Alberta, where the infamous American whiskey trading post Fort Whoop-Up, near Lethbridge, had devastated the Blackfoot. The federal government established the North-West Mounted Police (NWMP) in 1873. The original troop of 275 Mounties left Dufferin, Manitoba on July 8, 1874. They arrived north of present-day Bow Island, along the South Saskatchewan River, on September 9th, the 64th day of their long ride west.

Weeks later, after a detour south to Montana to resupply, the NWMP reached an empty Fort Whoop-Up in Lethbridge, recently abandoned by the American whiskey traders. That fall, the Mounties set up headquarters in Fort MacLeod, 49 kilometres west of Lethbridge.

Captain James Palliser, who led a British survey expedition through Canada's west during the late 1850s, found that much of southern Alberta, Saskatchewan, and Manitoba was too dry to support agriculture. Despite his warnings, the federal government promoted the area's settlement to immigrant farmers. This semi-arid region became known as Palliser's Triangle.

The first settlers in southern Alberta were ranchers in the late 1880s, who grazed their cattle over the grasslands of much of the fence-less region. Slowly, homesteading farmers joined them as the Canadian Pacific Railway laid its steel roadway across the prairies on its way to British Columbia.

It wasn't until 1900 that the first settlers arrived in the Bow Island area. Fifty-year-old Nathan Wallwork, originally from England, and his son-in-law, Ben Whitney, set out from Lethbridge with two horse teams loaded with lumber, to establish ranches north of the present-day town near the South Saskatchewan River. They followed the railway tracks across the featureless prairie to find their way. At first, they built a pair of one-room shacks, replacing them with a real house in 1903.

Ultimately, the Canadian Pacific Railway founded Bow Island. The first permanent resident was a CPR foreman, a Swede named James Olquist, who moved there in June, 1903, when the railway decided to create a section house at the location. His initial home was a boxcar without wheels. One year later, James built the community's first homestead, near the railway tracks—a small shack that still stood well into the 1970s.

The CPR was also responsible for choosing the ironic name "Bow Island" for the dusty, land-locked locality. It is thought that the community was named after an island north of the nearby community of Grassy Lake, which is located where the Bow and Oldman rivers join to become the South Saskatchewan River.

Popular legend in the community, though, adds a twist to the naming saga. It suggests Bow Island was actually to be named Grassy Lake, for a large slough that existed at the time south of town, and that Grassy Lake, which lies near that island in the middle of the Bow and Oldman rivers, was to be named Bow Island. It lays responsibility for the naming mix-up on the CPR for driving the wrong naming stakes in the ground in the two communities.

Bow Island quickly grew. People flocked to the community to serve the needs of homesteaders who began to settle in the district. By 1906, Bow Island had a post office. The Bell brothers started the first store in 1907, followed closely by others, including Chinese immigrant Chuck Chuen's combined store/restaurant called the Queen's Cafe.

In 1909, the community had three hotels, four general stores, a livery stable, its first school, and a baseball team. That summer saw the arrival of its first doctor, a Dr. Thomas Robert Ross, a graduate of Queen's University. He set up a private hospital in a former two-storey grocery store, with his offices downstairs and living quarters for himself, his wife, and two nurses upstairs.

Three years later, on March 12, 1912, the village officially became a town with a population pushing past 300 people. Bow Island was soon on the map for a huge natural gas well called Old Glory, originally developed by the CPR in February, 1909 to power its water pump house on the South Saskatchewan River.

Old Glory became famous for two reasons: its abundance of natural gas, and for catching fire in the summer of 1909 and burning so spectacularly for so many months that it was reported in newspapers throughout the United States. It burned so brightly that, at night, Walter Caswell's family could read the headlines of a newspaper on their farm nearly two miles away. At the time, Old Glory was the biggest producer of natural gas in Canada. Bow Island became known as "the town that lights the west."

In 1913, the town's second-ever private hospital opened on the ground floor of Cote Lodging, a two-storey boarding house. Dr. John Harwood Paterson, a graduate of McGill University, started the hospital. Dr. Paterson lost his 28-year-old wife in 1918 during the influenza epidemic and the hospital closed. Bow Island would not have a hospital again for more than 40 years.

The town continued to progress and by 1921 had a population of 427. Nothing would stand in its way until the Great Depression and the Dirty 30s, whose trials live on in the memories of local people who survived the repeated crop failures and howling dust storms. Bow Island would lose one-fourth of its residents and not claw its way back to its pre-Depression era population until 1946, when the census records 432 residents.

By the time Dr. Harry Nikaido arrived in the Spring of 1951, Bow Island residents had dusted themselves off and were on the road to bigger and better things. The 1950s were "hellish good years" for growing wheat on the area's dry-land farms, according to long-time farmer George Thacker, and the introduction of irrigation farming, just on the horizon, would profoundly improve local agriculture.

No words better express a sense of the prairies, and of prairie dwellers, than those by Wallace Stegner in his autobiography, *Wolf Willow*, about growing up in the nearby Cypress Hills.

*"The world is very large, the sky even larger and you are very small. But also the world is flat, empty, nearly abstract and in its flatness you are a challenging upright thing, as sudden as the exclamation mark, as enigmatic as a question mark.*

*"It is a country to breed mystical people, egocentrical people. But not humble ones. At noon the total sun pours on your single head; at sunrise and sunset you throw a shadow a hundred yards long ... Puny you may feel there, and vulnerable, but not unnoticed. This is a land to mark the sparrow's fall."*

**This is a photo of downtown Bow Island in 1910, complete with a team of oxen and a team of horses. (Photo courtesy of the Esplanade Arts and Heritage Centre Archives)**

A bird's eye view of Bow Island taken in the early 1900s with the railway station in the foreground to the right. By March 12, 1912 the growing community had officially become a town with a population of more than 300 people. (Photo courtesy of the Esplanade Arts and Heritage Centre Archives)

# CHAPTER 7
## Doc Chooses Bow Island

Southern Alberta was a sea of melting ice in March 1951, courtesy of a warm chinook wind that defrosted the frigid countryside after a severe winter.

Dr. Harry Nikaido was 31 when he pulled up stakes in Saskatchewan and headed to Alberta to start a medical practice. The original destination of his western ramble is a matter of debate. Some say he was headed for Calgary or west of Calgary to the town of Cochrane. Others say he planned to hang his shingle in Bassano, a community on the Trans-Canada Highway, 160 kilometres northwest of Medicine Hat. Everyone agrees he was not bound for Bow Island.

He made it as far as Medicine Hat but got stranded by muddy roads and took refuge at the YMCA. Running short of cash, he hung around local bars and restaurants, killing time, and met people who became friends for life, including Bill Noviski and Don Fraser, a young farmer from Bow Island.

Doc made two attempts to head west from Medicine Hat toward Bassano and Calgary. The first time an impassible road stopped him and he returned to Medicine Hat. On the second try, his car broke down only a few kilometres out of the city, near the farm of George and Violet Lee. He stayed with the Lees while his car was repaired. While there, Doc heard that the farming community of Bow Island, 59 kilometres west of Medicine Hat on Highway 3, was looking for a doctor. Perhaps it was divine intervention or maybe simply fate, but on a whim he decided to open a practice in Bow Island.

He arrived in a community where a district health nurse provided the only medical service. There hadn't been a doctor for a half a dozen years or more, since World War II. The town had 650 residents and a small drug store selling patent medicine but no pharmacist, hospital, or ambulance service.

In 1951, Bow Island had no paved streets, neon signs, or traffic lights. The highway through the town had only been paved the previous year. There was no indoor skating or curling rink, no swimming pool, library, or liquor store. All of those services and facilities arrived a couple of years later, when the introduction of irrigation farming to the area doubled the population in a decade.

It was a town whose citizens included pioneers who had broken virgin soil and planted the first crops. Residents were the descendants of risk takers, second sons, displaced peasant farmers, the politically oppressed, and folks simply desperate for a fresh start. Pioneering creeds dominated: stoicism in the face of pain, life's trials, and weather's crushing blows; a fierce individualism tempered by a willingness to work communally to help neighbours and community; a passion for sports and respect for religion exceeding that for education or art.

It was a place where no one culture dominated. Its immigrants were from Germany and western Europe, Scandinavia, Great Britain, and the United States. Local customs, habits, politics, and religious observances were brought from the old country, sometimes to thrive anew, and sometimes to combine with others to make new traditions.

A man raised on Vancouver's Robson Street, with six years at U of T in downtown Toronto, found himself in a place where the handful of grain elevators hugging the rail tracks, the three-storey Myrtle Hotel, and a brick school were the closest thing to a skyscraper. It was so quiet at night that he could hear the howl of car tires passing on the highway from one end of town to the other.

Doc, who had smelled the salty tang of Vancouver Harbour from the steps of his boyhood home, was landlocked in a town 10 kilometres from the nearest water: the South Saskatchewan River. Raised in one of Canada's rainiest regions, he had moved to one of its driest: Canada's sunshine capital. Rain was so rare that, when it did come, children jumped on their bicycles and drove around in it for the pure joy. "Dry as a popcorn's fart," old timers say.

Unlike the mountain-rimmed Vancouver of his childhood, the land was a flat distance without limits under an unending sky.

He set up shop and residence in a small office on the main street, near the pharmacy. It was a few doors down from Chuen's, a grocery store run by Sun Chuen. Sun's father Chuck immigrated from Canton, China and founded Chuck Chuen Co. in 1909. A local institution, the family's generosity and unlimited credit sustained many farmers during the Dirty 30s.

The tiny store had three aisles so narrow that the hips of fleshier shoppers brushed against both sides. The shelves along the walls were packed to the tinned ceiling with dry and canned goods. A long wooden counter guarded a brass-plated cash register that looked to be the last survivor of a shootout at a 1920s speakeasy.

Living and working only a few doors down, Doc became one of their large family, and could often be found reading a newspaper or grabbing a snack at a table in the back room, which housed a stove, a butcher's block, and a hand-cranked meat slicer.

Doc, the Chuens, the Zhous, the Fukamis, and the Matsumotos were the only Asian-Canadians in town. A few Japanese-Canadian families, such as the Nishis and Nakatsurus, lived on farms in the surrounding district.

There were fewer than 3,000 Japanese-Canadians in southern Alberta in the early 1950s. Some were descendants of farm labourers and farmers who had moved to the Raymond-Hardieville area in the early 20th Century to raise sugar beets. Others descended from Japanese pioneers who came to the Lethbridge area to work in coal mines and build the railway. Many were the remainder of the 2,250 Japanese Canadians displaced from the B.C. coast during World War II and relocated to southern Alberta to work on sugar beet farms.

Doc settled in and was soon a fixture in Bow Island. A non-conformist, he appreciated that residents let him do his own thing in his way. He did what he liked when he liked. Doc remained the only physician in town until 1954, when Dr. Stephen Carr also opened a practice on the main street. In 1958, Dr. Stewart Woolner joined Carr's practice, but Doc, a lone wolf, continued to practise on his own.

Slowly, support grew in the town and surrounding county to build a hospital. As one of the physicians, Doc played an important role in pushing the idea. A provisional board was established and held a plebiscite in December 1955 to see whether taxpayers supported the idea. It passed with a large majority.

It was Bow Island's second attempt to build a public hospital. In 1912, the town's citizens set up a hospital board and went so far as to have architectural drawings done for a facility with two public wards and two private wards, but it was never built.

The Bow Island Hospital officially opened on February 12, 1959. The one-storey facility had an operating room, delivery room, eight two-bed wards and four single-bed units, an eight-bassinet nursery, an x-ray and laboratory department, dining room, and doctor's room. Nearby was a 10-bed nurses' residence.

Almost 900 people attended the official opening, more than three-quarters of the town's population, to see nurse matron Frances Gerwing cut the ribbon as hospital chairman A.J. "Gus" Bonette, a driving force behind the hospital's establishment, looked on. Despite the cold, people lined up to tour the new facility, with the last visitors staying past 5 p.m.

It was Alberta's 104th hospital and the 37th the province had built since World War II, fuelled in part by the province's rising oil royalties. Bow Island's newspaper of the time, *The Graphic*, celebrated the special occasion with an eight-page hospital section. It glowingly described the hospital's details from the "bright rose chesterfields and three gold leather easy chairs" in the waiting room, to the east and south facing solarium, a "very comfortable place for the up-patients to read, visit or listen to the radio."

Doc was pleased to finally have a hospital.

"A doctor without a hospital is like a mechanic without a garage," he told his friend George Lee.

Four grain elevators hug the rail line in Bow Island in
this photo taken in the 1970s. There are no longer any
elevators standing in the town proper. (Photo courtesy
of the Esplanade Arts and Heritage Centre Archives)

# CHAPTER 8
## Doc The Doctor – Going The Extra Mile

The dogged determination, intelligence, and indifference to convention and authority that marked Harry Nikaido's early life, served him well as the young doctor matured into an experienced general practitioner. Patients loved his diligent care.

He went that extra mile, literally, especially in the early years when Bow Island had no hospital or ambulance service. Sometimes this involved bundling a sick patient into Doc's car in the middle of the night in bad weather and striking out for the nearest hospital in Medicine Hat, a 35-minute drive on narrow Highway 3.

In June, 1963, Doc escaped town to attend a wedding in Crowsnest Pass, in the shadow of the Rocky Mountains. As usual, he left the hospital a phone number to reach him in case of an emergency. The nurses called late in the evening's celebrations to tell him that Dolly Mellen's baby was coming early. Really early. Doc made the three-hour trip back, and without any sleep, delivered baby Shaun, more than two months early and weighing only two pounds, 12 ounces.

He put Shaun in an incubator, jumped in his car, and headed for Medicine Hat, followed by a vehicle carrying the new father, Fred Mellen, his mother, Mildred, and his mother-in-law, Viola Annon. Sleepy, Doc weaved from side to side on the narrow highway, hitting the gravelled shoulder and spitting rocks into the ditches lining both sides of the road.

"Doc! Stay awake you son of a bitch!" Mildred Mellen yelled from the trailing car, as if Doc could hear her. Somehow the entourage arrived safely at the hospital. Tiny Shaun survived and was released from hospital two months later.

Nine-year-old Beverley Fraser's acute appendicitis sent Doc on a similar late-night trip in the early 1960s, with her and mother Clara in the back seat of his car. Bev's two uncles followed in their vehicle, in case Doc's old beater broke down along the way to Medicine Hat, as it was known to do.

It was not unusual for Doc to make medical house calls over long distances to patients and friends, the two categories often indistinguishable. When good friend George Lee came down with viral pneumonia and was very ill, Doc drove more than 50 kilometres to his farm outside Medicine Hat to treat him.

"Doc gave me medication and stayed with me all the night and most of the morning," says George. "I think if he didn't come, I would have died. I was very, very sick."

Doc's house calls included the occasional planned home delivery, a rare occurrence in an era that prided itself on the modern efficiency of hospital births. Home births hearkened to pioneer days. The home birth movement in Canada was still years away.

Going the extra mile didn't only mean jumping in the car to take medical care to his patients. Doc often went above and beyond in the hospital setting.

Dixie Johnson, a former nurse, recalls Doc's diligent efforts when she had her son, Darren. She had hemorrhaged the month before and Doc was worried about placenta previa, which can cause vaginal bleeding and lead to other complications such as fetal distress. It also results in the need for a caesarean section. Doc stayed with her the whole night of her labour to make sure everything was okay.

On December 3, 1969, Mavis Weatherhead, then a nurse at the hospital, gave birth to her daughter, Tami. The delivery had gone okay, but Doc worried that the baby had congested lungs. For the next 48 hours, either lying on a stretcher beside Mavis or sprawled in a nearby chair, Doc kept vigil. Every time the baby started to turn blue, he gave the soles of her feet a flick with his fingers to get her crying to clear her lungs. After crying her lungs out, baby Tami was a healthy pink.

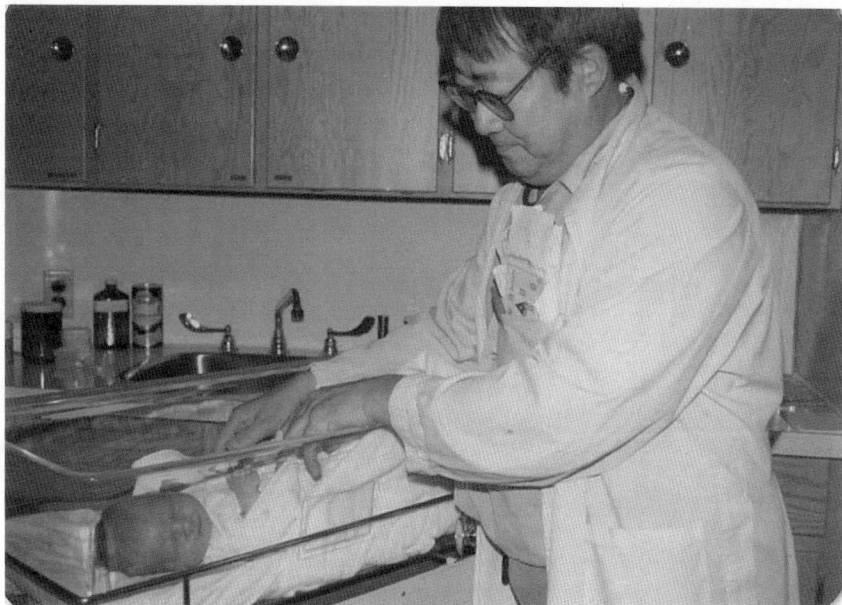

Doc checks out a newborn baby at the Bow Island Hospital in this undated photograph. Doc delivered more than 160 babies during his years of service to the community, including eight siblings from one family.

# CHAPTER 9
## Doc The Doctor – The Innovator

Harry Nikaido may have been a general practitioner in a rural setting, but he was not letting his skills rust. His nose was constantly in medical journals, reading about the latest developments and advances, and then applying them to meet the needs of his patients.

"He felt very alone in his practice in Bow Island," says retired nurse Sheila Bjerkseth. "He spent hours and hours with his medical books ... he did a lot of studying."

"Doc wasn't sitting back in the bushes," says retired nurse Heather Thacker. "He was out there trying to find better ways of doing stuff."

One unique approach was to give penicillin injections in an oil base, rather than in water. It was very thick. Patients often complained, because it didn't dissolve into the tissue right away, like water-based penicillin. Instead, it sat there in a lump. But it worked and was longer lasting.

Doc was a big proponent of penicillin. If you came to him with aches and chills, you were probably going to get a shot of penicillin. It may seem odd by today's standards, but there wasn't a lot in the antibiotic range in the 1950s, 1960s, and 1970s when Doc practised medicine.

Another favourite practice was to prescribe Nyacin-50 for elderly patients and those with circulation problems. Nyacin-50, essentially Vitamin B, dilates the small blood vessels and is good for arthritis, cholesterol, and overall heart health. It gives the patient a good, warm flush.

At the hospital, Doc performed minor surgeries, such as tonsillectomies and tooth extractions, often on Saturdays when the nursing matron was off and out of town. Before surgery, his patients gargled with diluted hydrogen peroxide to stop any bleeding and to avoid infections. It was not standard medical practice at the time, but is done today.

Necessity is the mother of invention and Doc was not above inventing a new medical contraption when necessary. Young farmer Randy Voss came to the hospital with a crush injury that turned his pointer finger right around. Normally such injuries required the patient to be sent to the city for orthopaedic surgery to have pins inserted. Voss, however, was getting married at the week's end and had more important things to do.

Doc put on his thinking cap. He asked for a Bunsen burner, a bone pin, a wire coat hanger, a good elastic band, and a wooden match. He wired together a great big gizmo that kept Voss's finger properly in place to heal. The result pleased the future groom.

In its early years, the Bow Island Hospital didn't have a defibrillator—an electrical device to restore normal heartbeat through brief electric shock. They were relatively new and expensive. Officially the hospital didn't have one. However, underneath Doc's desk in the doctor's room sat a homemade one. Doc used two spoons, some wire, and a battery to build it, although he never put it to use.

# CHAPTER 10
## Doc At Play

Doc worked long hours for more than two decades but managed to take the occasional break to shed his responsibilities. In the early years, Doc tried to visit Calgary for a couple of days a month, usually staying with friend Hugh Louis and his wife, Anne. In the summer and fall, he drove up to catch CFL football games at McMahon Stadium, watching quarterback Jerry Keeling and tight end Herm Harrison on the Calgary Stampeders of the 1950s and 1960s.

"He'd go up to the Stampeders' games, and sometimes, he didn't come back when he said he would," says Linda Volk, who worked as his part-time receptionist for two summers as a teenager.

Often, he simply visited the city to hang around with Hugh and his Chinese-Canadian friends and "chew the fat". Doc didn't like to socialize with the few Japanese-Canadians living in the city in the 1950s and early 1960s, as he didn't speak Japanese. He enjoyed eating in Chinatown, where his favourite spot was the New China Restaurant on Centre Street.

"He kind of missed the social life in the city," says Hugh, "although, if he had patients, there's no way he left them. When he came to Calgary, he left my phone number at the hospital and if there were any problems ... the matron at the hospital phoned here."

In Bow Island, if Doc wasn't dropping in on friends for supper or a visit in his off time, he often spent it playing or watching sports as he had since he was a boy. The sports he played in Alberta were not the soccer and lacrosse he excelled at in B.C. and Toronto, nor the rugby and water polo he played at university. He took up golf, as well as baseball and softball and also curling—a Western Canadian passion.

An outstanding athlete in the past, Doc did not excel in any of these newly adopted sports. He was in his early 30s, gaining weight, and working punishingly long hours, and so no longer dominated the playing fields as he had in his youth. His physical prowess diminishing, he became a student of the games and studied their strategies.

Golf became Doc's passion. He spent much of his time at the nine-hole course only two blocks from the hospital, practising chip shots and looking for golf balls. Doc had hundreds of used balls rolling around in the front and back seat of his car, and ice cream buckets full of them in the trunk. The old timers in town called golf "cow patty pool", hearkening back to the original golf course, northwest of town, which was a cow pasture.

Doc was an ardent golfer, if not a great one, but as a perfectionist, he was always trying to improve his game, especially his iron shots. He hit right-handed and was a bogey golfer, celebrating any par or birdie.

His love of golf was well known at the hospital. Veteran nurses were so familiar with Doc's routine that they knew how long he took to play the course and could often guess which hole he should be on when they needed to find him. It wasn't uncommon to see a young nurse, in her starched, white uniform and nurse's cap, wandering the course looking to bring Doc back for an emergency. Some nurses signalled that he was needed by lowering the hospital's flag to half mast. A nurse's aide sent to find Doc to fill a prescription returned with it written on Doc's cigarette package.

One day, a young mother arrived at the hospital with her recently circumcised baby boy. While cleaning him, she had retracted his foreskin and couldn't pull it back. The baby's tiny penis was getting redder and redder. Doc was needed but was in the middle of a golf tournament and didn't want to leave. He sent word back to the hospital to ice the baby's penis and for the family to bring the baby out to the course so he could have a look.

During Doc's 24 years in Bow Island, the golf course was a dry and rutted layout with few trees. It had the oiled, sand greens common in small Prairie communities of the time. Renovations that installed grass greens, more trees, sand bunkers, and underground sprinklers were years away.

When Doc wasn't practising his game with retired elevator agent Cecil McNeely, the two could often be seen burning off the course's stubbly yellow grass that crunched under foot, in the hope of encouraging greener shoots among the wind-blown yellow grass.

Baseball was one of the first popular local sports Doc picked up, in an area known for producing good ballplayers. Teams like the Bow Island-Burdett Combines dominated various southern Alberta senior leagues from 1948 to 1968.

Doc joined a team nicknamed the Burdett Alcoholics, which played against neighbouring communities on dusty ball fields riddled with gopher holes. Trapped tumbleweeds writhed in the chicken wire fences protecting the ball diamonds. Most of the players were farmers, and in early days, the bases were often metal discs from a seeder. He played catcher, outfield, or first base. Not a great fielder or much of a batter, he knew the rulebook inside out and was a fierce competitor.

Spectators got a kick out of watching a doctor playing ball. They didn't hesitate to give him some good-natured heckling, in a community where everyone on the bleachers knew everyone on the ball diamond.

"Doc, have patience," they yelled, laughing as Doc argued a strike called by the umpire.

In the winter, Doc switched to curling. The Bow Island curling rink is a small, Quonset-style building with a semi-circular roof line, adjacent to its larger twin, the arena. Merle Nelson, who with his twin brother, Vern, often curled with Doc, says he approached the game as intensely as a professional, but didn't possess the matching skills.

"Doc, you see my broom?" Vern often admonished Doc from the rings, when pointing out a shot that Doc had missed. "You're supposed to aim at it."

Sometimes Doc made the more than three-hour trip to Calgary to curl in bonspiels with Hugh and his friends. Doc usually demanded to skip any team he played on.

"He has to skip. He's read the book you know," says Clara Fraser, whose husband, Don, curled with Doc for many years.

Although Doc was no curling champion, he talked a good game. He sat in the spectator area looking out on the three sheets of ice and offered running commentary. Later, at the hospital, he regaled nurses with shot-by-shot breakdowns of every rock thrown through every end of one game or another—whether they wanted to hear it or not.

If Doc couldn't be found at the curling rink or a friend's house in his off hours, he was likely in a corner seat in the town's only bar at the Myrtle Hotel, reading a newspaper, with his glasses down at the end of his nose. The bar at the Myrtle, built in 1909 and named after the first baby born in the area, was dark and windowless with terry-towel-covered round tables, a jar of ancient pickled eggs on the bar, and a juke box in the corner. Two doors led inside from the street, one marked by a sign overhead for Men, the other for Ladies and Escorts.

It was scandalous for the doctor to spend a few hours there, even though all Doc usually had in front of him was a Coke or a glass of draft beer that he lingered over for the night. He had the occasional beer, but few people, if any, ever saw him close to intoxicated. He was nearly always on call and could never let his guard down.

One time, a fight broke out between two men at a nearby table while Doc was sitting in the bar after a hard day. The battle royale amused him, but he halted it for a moment to ensure both combatants were not seriously injured.

"Okay, go back at it," he said, once he was sure no serious harm was being done.

From time to time, proper older ladies (who would never otherwise set foot in the bar) were forced to drop in to pick up their medications from Doc, if he had already closed his office for the day.

The Myrtle and Alex Zhou's adjacent café were both Doc's living rooms, places where he hung out to relax, talk, and read. And if people didn't approve of him spending time at the bar, he wouldn't hesitate to tell them to get stuffed.

The Myrtle Hotel, both its café and the tavern, were favourite haunts where Doc could be found when not working. At the bar, he was usually sitting in a corner seat, reading a newspaper. The same glass of beer might sit in front of him all night. (Photo courtesy of the Esplanade Arts and Heritage Centre Archives)

Doc is pictured in the uniform of the Burdett Huskies baseball team in this photo taken in the early 1960s. The team's nickname for themselves was the Alcoholics. Doc also played softball and curled but his real passion was golf.

# CHAPTER 11
## Doc The Doctor – The Master Diagnostician

Doc had a reputation, among his medical peers in southern Alberta, as a skilled diagnostician with an uncanny ability to diagnose the problem and a fierce determination to find the solution. One patient described it almost spiritually.

"When he heard what you were saying, it was almost like it was part of him," says former nurse's aide and patient Rosella Hadnagy. "He knew what he was going to do to fix the problem."

Once in diagnostic mode, Doc was totally engaged. He carefully listened as the patient described her condition and ailment, examined her for signs and symptoms, and utilized the limited diagnostic procedures available to him.

"One of his strengths was his bulldog mentality," says Sheila Bjerkseth. "He worked until he found out what was happening … and he did everything to find the solution."

It wasn't unusual for doctors to call from Medicine Hat and other communities to seek his opinion. Most of Bow Island's nursing staff were his patients. Former patients and friends say his diagnostic skills were so respected that Calgary's Foothills Hospital unsuccessfully tried to woo him.

Bill and Marilyn Noviski credited Doc with saving the life of their one-year-old boy Norman. Doc was called in for an assessment after doctors at the Medicine Hat Hospital were unable to figure out why Norman was convulsing and turning blue. Doc determined that he had water on the brain and ordered a spinal tap to remove the pressure.

The accuracy of his diagnoses were no doubt helped by his having been physician to many of his patients' for much, if not all, of their lives. Doc knew them in their "well" state. As a small town doctor always up to date on local gossip, he was aware of their professional and personal lives and the potential impact these had on their health.

Fred Mellen's young daughter Mickey was having problems, which Doc soon diagnosed as nephritis, an inflammation of the kidneys and potentially life-threatening. Doc sent her to Medicine Hat to see a specialist for a long series of tests and examinations, which came to the same conclusion. The specialist was surprised that Doc was able to come up with the diagnosis so quickly, given the limited tools at his disposal. Mickey finally came home after spending 38 days in the hospital.

Friend Ella Nelson says a parlour trick Doc enjoyed was to diagnose the illnesses of actors on TV based on what he saw on the small screen. In one particular case, he diagnosed an actor as suffering from Grave's disease, an autoimmune disease that commonly affects the thyroid. Sure enough, his diagnosis was confirmed months later in the newspaper.

Like any professional, and despite being a good doctor, Doc occasionally made mistakes or had his professional capabilities questioned. In the spring of 1961, Medicine Hat coroner Dr. E.G.F. Skinner was called to investigate the death of a three-year-old Medicine Hat boy during a tonsillectomy performed by Doc at the Bow Island Hospital with the help of an anaesthetist. Doc was not found to be negligent.

What differentiated him from other doctors of the time was his willingness to admit mistakes.

Dixie Johnson says that one day she brought in her son to be examined by Doc, because he had a cyst on his arm. Doc immediately referred him to a specialist in Calgary out of fear that the cyst was cancer. Later it was found not to be cancerous. Doc felt bad for unnecessarily alarming Dixie.

"He was very apologetic and said he'd missed reading a page in the medical textbook," says Dixie.

It was not only Doc's diagnostic skills that were his strength. He also had a common sense approach to treatment and an ability to communicate. On Tom and Coreen Thacker's first wedding anniversary, Tom became very ill. The couple went to see Doc, who diagnosed Tom with a kidney stone.

Doc's prescription was for Coreen to drink plenty of water and every time she had a glass, Tom was to have one quart of water with baking soda in it to help soften and possibly dissolve the kidney stone. Doc's treatment was successful and it was 40 years before Tom was troubled with a kidney stone again.

Today a doctor would likely prescribe plenty of fluids and pain medicine for small stones and either surgery or high-energy shock wave therapy to break the stones, for those that do not pass by themselves.

Doc's reputation as a physician spread far enough that it wasn't uncommon for patients to come from as far as Calgary for treatment, especially Chinese Canadians, particularly those with skin disorders. Doc developed his own salve to help them.

"I think they thought they were coming to the Mayo Clinic," says Coreen, who was a nurse at the Bow Island Hospital.

# CHAPTER 12
## House Calls

Unlike many physicians, Doc liked to make house calls, but with Doc that didn't necessarily mean a visit to offer medical expertise—although he made that kind of visit too.

It wasn't unusual for him to pop in out of the blue at the homes of friends and patients in the Bow Island area, and even those closer to Medicine Hat, 50 kilometres away. He would stroll in at supper time and demand to know what was cooking. If cooking hadn't begun, he didn't hesitate to suggest that steak would be nice. He loved steak.

Doc had a voracious appetite and always welcomed second helpings. He ate anything. He was known to walk through a house and out the back door to pluck onions and radishes from the garden to make a sandwich. Or to grab some mashed or boiled potatoes and stick them between two slabs of bread.

Like most men of his generation, Doc didn't help clean up dishes after the meal. He headed for the living room and took command of the television, preferring to watch sports if there were any games on, or read the newspaper. By the end of the evening, Doc was likely asleep on the living room floor in front of the TV, snoring loudly, with a newspaper over his head. It's where he stayed until late in the night or early morning, when he woke and let himself out, unless the hospital had already telephoned and reeled him back in to work.

He spent many nights with the Henningsgard family. Bud Henningsgard was a good friend, and his mother, Olga, an original homesteader in the nearby Burdett area, was one of his first patients when he arrived in town. Doc visited Bud and family two or three times a week. The first thing he said as he walked in the door was "got anything to eat?" Bud's wife, Dora, always put a plate in the fridge for Doc, because he might show up at any time, even at 4 a.m..

Saturday evenings would often find Doc at the Henningsgard's watching Hockey Night in Canada. Doc had to fight with the family's 15-pound tomcat for his favourite chair. Doc would carry on a conversation, watch the game, and read the newspaper at the same time. If Doc had a minor surgery the next day, he practised tying surgical knots—left-handed, right-handed, left-handed, right-handed ... over and over while he watched.

Doc mixed visits with a bit of doctoring, if required. Once he decided to give the Henningsgard's youngest son, Del, a shot of penicillin to help ward off the tonsillitis that was always troubling him. Del saw Doc coming with the needle and promptly dived under his bed. Doc headed under the bed too and Del got his needle.

Sometimes Doc stopped in at Don and Clara Fraser's farmhouse, outside Bow Island. On occasion he used their kitchen to cook a meal for the Frasers and their two daughters, usually western-style Chinese food. Afterward the kitchen looked as if it had been ransacked by raccoons, as he would use every pot in the place.

He was always talkative when he visited. He was well read, up on the latest gossip, and very opinionated. He was witty and loved to laugh when among people he knew. There was nothing he liked more than watching old black and white movies on TV. He knew every movie and didn't hesitate to tell everyone what was going to happen, regardless of whether they had seen it or not.

When he wanted to get away from the "rat race" in Bow Island, he visited Merle and Ella Nelson in Burdett, 10 kilometres away. Sometimes he stayed for days and set up medical practice in their living room, with patients coming from as far away as Medicine Hat—a 40-minute drive.

He often visited Bill and Marilyn Noviski in Seven Persons, where he would bring every one of the family's magazines into the bathroom, creating an impromptu library. One day when he came to visit, Marilyn was out at a neighbour's for coffee. Supper hour was approaching and Doc was hungry. Growing impatient, he called the neighbour's house and asked her to tell Marilyn to come home, because her children were hungry. The Noviski children, Dalyce and Norman, were actually at their aunt's place for the night. It was only Doc who was starving.

Norman remembers Doc arriving with his golf clubs and teeing off into the neighbour's summer fallow, while Norman was tasked with retrieving the balls. Afterward Doc and Bill, a steam engineer at the Medicine Hat power plant, would sit at the table all night and discuss a wide range of subjects, since they shared a similar degree of intellectual curiosity.

It wasn't unusual for the Lees, who lived down the road from the Noviskis, to wake up on the weekend on their farm and see Doc sleeping in his car in the farm yard, feet sticking out of the side window. Violet and George, whose father came to Canada from China in the late 1800s to help build the railways, were a mixed marriage, which was rare in southern Alberta in the 1950s and 1960s.

Doc might spend the entire day simply punting a football back and forth across their yard with George's younger brother. He berated Violet if she had cleaned out the bottom of the rice pot since his last visit, because he liked the crust at the bottom. So when she cleaned out the bowl, Violet stored the crust in the freezer and thawed it out for Doc to eat on visits.

One Christmas season saw Doc invited to the nearby community of Conquerville for a Christmas party and to spend the night at a friend's house. The next morning he ate two steaks for breakfast before he and another friend hit the road to take up half a dozen dinner and party invitations for the day. He ate his fill at every stop.

Another unusually mild Christmas, Donald and Donna Jenkins invited Doc to dinner at their farm south of Bow Island. Afterward, Doc found the small farmhouse too hot, crowded, and noisy for an after-meal nap and so headed to the barn's hayloft to catch a few winks. He told the Jenkins to wake him up if the hospital called with an emergency, because the nurses on duty had the phone number. They always had his number. On the fourth call from the now insistent nurses, Donald reluctantly woke up Doc. Harry Nikaido's Christmas break was over.

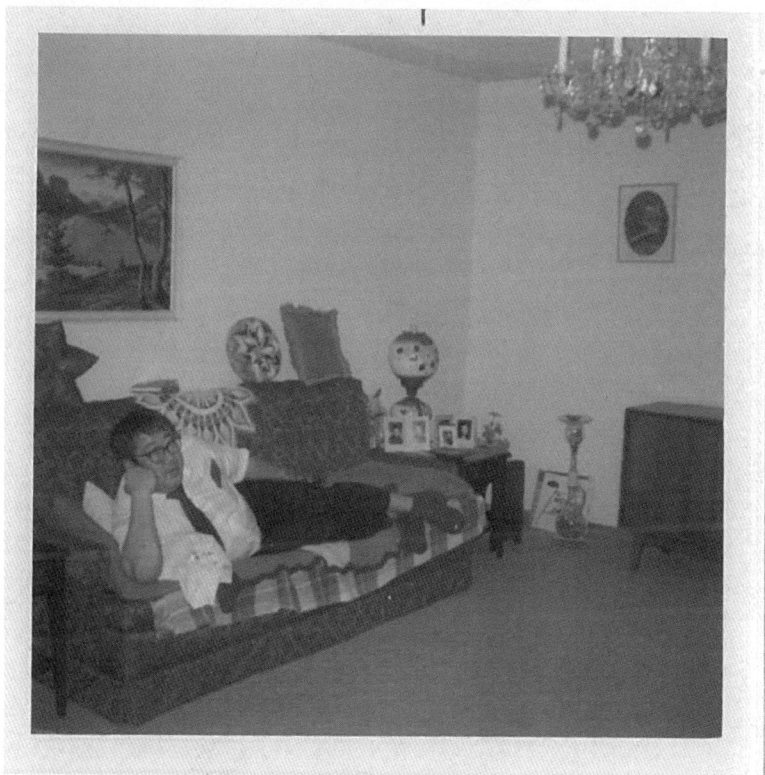

Doc rests comfortably on a friend's couch on one of his housecalls. Friends and patients say it wasn't unusual for the bachelor doctor to drop in, unannounced, for supper and then stay to watch TV for the evening.

# CHAPTER 13
## Doc The Doctor – Professional Detachment

In the 1940s, the University of Toronto, like all medical schools, drilled the importance of professional detachment into students like Harry Nikaido, from their first anxious moments handling human cadavers to their immersion in the deep waters of clinical practice.

Professional detachment was felt to be necessary, to ensure doctors could objectively listen to their patients' describe their ailments, and after diagnosis, prescribe potentially intimate and painful procedures to cure them. Such detachment also enabled doctors to deliver life-altering news when required.

The medical profession believed that an important part of professional detachment was the necessity to limit the personal or non-professional involvement of physicians with their patients.

Given Doc's reputation as a diagnostician, he was clearly able to keep objective and observant of patients, even those he had brought into this world or looked after for decades.

As time went on in Bow Island though, the chalk line separating the doctor from patients and community became faded and blurred beyond recognition. Doc's friends were his patients and patients were friends. He ate and slept in their homes and joined in their parties and celebrations before seeing them the next day at his office or on the operating table.

Other small-town physicians of the time faced the same challenge, but usually with a spouse, family, or medical partner to be their confidant.

Doc had none of that. He was often the lone doctor or one of only two serving Bow Island and the entire County of Forty Mile—1,200-square kilometres stretching northward from the Montana border—with nearly 3,000 residents.

Over time, that combination of limited backup and his sense of responsibility to his patients, and to all the area's residents, chained Doc to the community. Perhaps a prison of his own making in some ways and yet a prison.

From time to time Doc managed to escape for a few free hours around town, to Medicine Hat for an afternoon or evening or to Calgary. On one of his visits to Calgary, a female patient in Bow Island died. George Lee says Doc felt badly about that incident for the rest of his life.

Over his 24 years of practice the list of deaths inevitably grew, as did Doc's sense of responsibility for those remaining.

**Doc, right, at a party with Ev Hall, an unidentified woman and Edie Hall in this undated photo. Many of Doc's friends were his patients and his patients were his friends.**

# CHAPTER 14
## Doc Fights The Tax Man

On February 24, 1942, five days before Harry Nikaido's 22nd birthday, the federal Cabinet authorized the internment of "all persons of Japanese racial origin" and forced their evacuation from the British Columbia coast.

The Nikaido family lost everything that his immigrant parents had worked to achieve. His brother and sister, Geri and Frank, were tossed out of the University of British Columbia.

Ottawa's decision confused Harry. He couldn't understand why he and his siblings—Canadian citizens, like 75 per cent of those of Japanese ancestry in Canada in 1941—were caught in this web of paranoia. That his parents, who had lived in Canada since the First World War, were trapped and being treated like criminals, bewildered him.

"He saw himself very much as a Canadian growing up, of Japanese ancestry," says friend Robin Dann. "When the war broke out, it was everyone else who saw him as Japanese. It was imposed on him in a negative way."

Harry never forgot the federal government's actions and never forgave Ottawa for its treatment of his family. He acted on that anger by launching a counterinsurgency of sorts against Ottawa, best described as tax warfare. Harry hit the government where it hurt, in the pocketbook, by trying not to pay any income tax.

"Why should I pay those sons of bitches any money after what they took from our family?" Doc asked Robin.

Alex Zhou remembers similar words from Doc.

"The Government got enough money from my parents," Doc said to Alex.

Alex is convinced to this day that Doc never paid income tax—ever.

"Doc was bound and determined not to pay taxes," says Robin. "In Bow Island, he had a thriving medical practice that could've made him wealthy, but he lived in poverty. He would rather live in poverty than pay taxes to a government he despised for their treatment of his family."

Doc's resistance took many forms, from active to passive. One approach was to limit his reportable income. He charged patients little for appointments—a few dollars at most, certainly far less than the going rates in the years before Medicare—and rarely filed Medicare claims after universal health care was implemented.

Another approach was to try to conceal what little income he did make. He was careful not to make too many bank deposits. He gave nurse Coreen Thacker a duffel bag full of one dollar bills and asked her to make a deposit in his account. Another time, he asked patient and friend Donna Jenkins to go to the bank for him in an effort not to leave tracks that the Revenue Canada bloodhounds could follow.

"He went out to his car and got some money from underneath the floorboards that was all dirty," says Donna.

Ironically, efforts to reduce his earnings only made his tax troubles worse. Even when he did file taxes, which was infrequently, his reported income was so low that Revenue Canada didn't believe it, given that he was the physician of record to half the people living in Bow Island and the surrounding County of Forty Mile.

One year, Doc told friend Hugh Louis: "I'm going to have to claim I made more money that I actually did." When Hugh asked why, Doc said it was because Revenue Canada didn't believe that he made so little.

At one point in the early 1970s, Doc told hospital administrator John Nicolet that Revenue Canada was assessing him for taxes based on what the average doctor in Alberta made, even though his actual income was far less.

If Revenue Canada would've asked, old timers in town would have told the federal tax men to give up chasing Doc for what little money he had. As they used to say, "You can't take the pants off a bare bum."

Sometimes Doc literally hid from the tax man. He would get telephone calls from local residents whenever anyone saw a suspicious-looking bureaucrat in town who might be from Revenue Canada. Doc ducked under his car out back of his office and pretended to be a mechanic doing a bit of work until the agent left. Other times he went to visit friends in the countryside, like Bill Noviski, until the tax man left.

Dalyce Bergen, Bill's daughter, remembers Doc showing up at their farm house and sleeping on the couch at the same time of year for many years, whenever the income tax people came looking for him.

A number of times in the mid-1960s and early 1970s, Doc hired young women to organize his finances and complete old Medical Services Insurance (MSI)—or Medicare—claim forms for payment. At least three women took on this Herculean task during a 10-year period, with little success. All had the sense that he embarked on the effort half-heartedly, because he was being pressured to get his financial house in order and wanted to be seen to be making the attempt.

"He was being hounded by MSI to submit his reports, because they had no way of tracking income tax for him or anything and they wanted to get a grasp on what he was making," says Linda Volk, who worked part-time for Doc in the late 1960s.

"In order to get them off his back, he hired me and I went through the back files, some going back seven years and coded everything. And the idea was, he was supposed to submit them, but he never did. For all the work I did, he never filed them, but he could say that he'd done them," says Linda, the daughter of Donna and Donald Jenkins.

Janice Goodfellow attempted the same thing for Doc in the summer of 1970, with the same result. Goodfellow says her sense was that getting his MSI records in order was something that Doc had been told to do but that he was just going through the motions.

"I didn't get a sense that he ever filed the forms we filled out," says Janice, the daughter of Doc's patients George and Florence Thacker.

Yet another weapon Doc used to battle Revenue Canada was confusion. Former local MLA Alan Hyland says Doc often filed tax forms that had been done incorrectly to avoid being charged with refusing to file.

"I file; I just don't file right," Doc told Alan.

Alan says, "Doc told me that he'd write on the forms to Revenue Canada that 'you know more about my business than I do.'"

It is not clear whether Doc paid some taxes or no taxes over the 24 years he practised medicine in Bow Island, or whether he ever filed any complete income tax returns. It may never be known.

An Access to Information request to the Canada Revenue Agency, formerly Revenue Canada, for records of any charges or convictions against Dr. Harry Nikaido for tax evasion or failure to file tax returns was unsuccessful. Any such files, if there ever were any, no longer exist.

What is clear is that Doc was in a running battle with Ottawa and Revenue Canada. It was a war that many of his patients, friends, and colleagues knew about. The local RCMP knew too.

Two Mounties who served in Bow Island in the early 1970s say Doc ran into trouble with Revenue Canada a number of times over that period and received at least three summonses to appear in court for failing to file income taxes. Wayne Barnes, a young constable in his second posting, says his supervisor, Corporal Jim Black, gave him the impression that Doc's tax troubles were an annual affair.

Constable Barry Dilts, who served in the community from 1972 to 1975, became friends with Doc, even though Doc hated Mounties because of their involvement in the evacuation of Japanese Canadians. Barry helped Doc deal with the summonses by writing Revenue Canada letters promising to file the income tax forms.

"I wrote the letters and he signed them and when you do that, you are making an effort to deal with them and they don't charge you," says Barry.

There is no record of Doc going to court to face tax charges until 1973. For some reason, that year Doc's tax problems, which he had always seemed to dodge, turned out differently.

It was March 1, 1973, and most of Doc's friends and patients, nurses and hospital staff gathered at the Legion for a BBQ dinner to celebrate Doc's 22 years of service to the community and his 53rd birthday. Friends, patients, and dignitaries made speeches, offered toasts, and showered Doc with gifts.

An off-duty Mountie among the crowd was enjoying the evening less than the other revellers as he had an arrest warrant for the man of the hour in his pocket.

Robin Dann witnessed a bizarre discussion unfold. The Mountie urged Doc to file something to Revenue Canada, anything, so that he could make the summons go away. Doc was noncommittal. At one point, businessman Ralph Bateman overheard the conversation and offered to help Doc with his tax problem.

Doc said he couldn't find the tax files in question and gave the lame excuse that he thought that they may have fallen off his bicycle when he was on his way to the hospital one night. Besides, he didn't have time to file something soon as he was in a golf tournament the following weekend and had a busy week ahead.

Forty years later, neither Barry nor Wayne recall attending Doc's Recognition Night or whether their supervisor, the late Corporal Jim Black, attended.

Wayne does remember arresting Doc on a charge a few weeks later. He didn't take Doc into custody, but served him the summons outside the Myrtle Hotel café. Doc was to appear in court for failing to file his 1971 tax return. Months earlier Doc had fixed up Wayne's hand after it got trapped in the door of a police cruiser. Doc didn't give the young constable a hard time about being served. Wayne says he had more of a "here we go again" response.

Doc was charged on April 9, 1973 with unlawfully failing to file his T1 1971 income tax return as required under Section 126(2) of the Income Tax Act and contrary to Section 238(2) of the Income Tax Act. He appeared in Provincial Court, sitting in Bow Island at a community hall, before Judge E.W.N. "Skip" MacDonald, serving out of Medicine Hat.

Doc's inclination was to fight the charge, but Barry and others convinced him to plead guilty. If Doc pleaded guilty, local justice officials could handle the case, but if he fought the charge, a federal Crown prosecutor would be brought in and the outcome might be harsher.

Dr. Harry Nikaido plead guilty to failing to file his 1971 tax return on June 11, 1973. One month later, in *The 40-Mile County Commentator*, buried halfway down in a summary of court news (among fines for teens with illegal alcohol possession, operating cars without tail lights, and drunk driving) was the following: "Dr. H. Nikaido was fined $200 and costs for failing to file an Income Tax return." In comparison, the same court fined a drunk driver caught driving without a licence a total of $300. In today's dollars, Doc's fine was about $1,100.

The conviction, fine, and local notoriety didn't upset Doc in the least. He laughed about it and told a colleague it was "a farce." It remains the only known record of Doc not paying taxes—or at least not filing his tax returns. He was served at least one more summons on tax issues in the early 1970s, but it never went to court.

As to why Revenue Canada didn't more aggressively prosecute Doc, no one knows. Perhaps friends and local officials were able to provide enough information to keep tax officials at bay. Maybe Doc's attempts to get his financial and MSI records in order bought time with Revenue Canada. Forty years later, John Nicolet offers an intriguing theory.

"Doc was a well-respected man in southern Alberta and my personal belief is that tax officials didn't want to open up a can of worms, in regards to him going into the story of how his family was affected during the war. It was a black mark in Canada's history and I think Doc had readied himself in case anybody would challenge him. He would explain why he was doing it, and because of his respected stature, I think officials backed off."

# CHAPTER 15
## The Mentor

On the surface, Doc did not strike anyone as a role model for youth, despite being a doctor and one of the few university-educated people in Bow Island.

He wasn't married and didn't own a home, or a bed for that matter. He wasn't a parent. He wasn't a churchgoer or a taxpayer, at least not if he could help it. He drove one wreck of a car after another. He could be gruff and abrupt, wasn't always a good listener in social company, and was fiercely opinionated. On the surface, he didn't appear to be a person inclined to go out of his way to help young people. But like everything to do with Doc, appearances were deceiving.

He took a number of teens and young adults under his wing, particularly bright ones. He urged them to set their sights beyond their home town. To leave the farm and get a university education, not common in southern Alberta in the 1950s and early 1960s, especially for young women.

Linda Volk spent two summers working part-time at Doc's office as a teenager. Doc sat down and talked to Linda about her future a number of times in the midst of the mess of his office. He urged her to go somewhere like Toronto and to make sure she went on to university. Linda went on to become a Registered Nurse at the Ponoka, Alberta General Hospital.

Rosella Hadnagy was a young nurse's aide in the early 1960s, learning her profession on the job at the Bow Island Hospital. Doc was patient with her as she learned the ropes and taught her a great deal.

"It was a teaching lesson every day and it wasn't like sitting in a class-room ... I received my training on the job and he was a very good teacher," she says.

Sometimes he helped the teenagers of patients and friends. He was close to Beverley and Carol, the daughters of Don and Clara Fraser, whose farmhouse he often visited. He treated Bev like a daughter, and as she got closer to high school graduation, was interested in her future plans. He talked to her about going to university and about what to expect there.

"For me and my sister, Carol, he encouraged us to do something, to get an education, as my parents did too," says Bev Walker, adding that wasn't common in the early 1970s in rural Alberta. "He wanted people to do their best."

Bev was considering a degree in the relatively new field of environmental science. Doc took a Socratic approach to discussing Bev's plans for university.

"His approach wasn't so much telling me what to do, it was more quizzing me about why I was thinking about environmental science versus something else. It was more like 'Okay, I want to know that you have thought about this in a robust way.' He really wasn't directive, it was 'Okay, environmental science, what do you think that might be?' Sort of testing me to see if I'd thought it through."

Bev decided to enrol in architecture instead of environmental science, but eventually switched faculties and graduated with a Commerce degree from the University of Alberta. While Doc's counselling for university was a good experience, his attempt to teach Bev how to golf when she was in Grade Nine was a disaster.

"We probably started out with 20 golf balls. He knew those golf balls and we had to keep looking until we found those exact 20 golf balls. It was really quite frustrating."

The teen Doc spent the most time with was Robin Dann, the son of a British-born, college-educated, United Church Minister/school teacher and a nurse's aide.

Not your typical small-town Prairie boy in the 1960s, Robin was a rabid reader, favouring George Orwell and George Bernard Shaw, histories and biographies. He enjoyed listening to Gilbert and Sullivan. At the age of 16, he travelled alone across Canada by train, before boarding a ship in

Montreal bound for Southampton, England. He travelled on to London to meet his parents who were on vacation.

Despite the nearly 30-years age difference, he and Doc got along famously. Robin enjoyed keeping up with current events, while Doc was a news hound, his pockets crammed with articles ripped out of newspapers and magazines. Both were sports fans, both free thinkers and bright. Robin started hanging out with the forty-something Doc when he was in his mid-teens, because "I liked him and he was a character." He appreciated Doc's cosmopolitan, Bohemian nature and keen intelligence. He liked that Doc had strong opinions and could converse on a number of topics "like a Renaissance man." Every once in a while, Doc teasingly told Robin he was a "dim-witted kid".

"I admired him and he put up with me," Robin says 40 years later, looking back on his friendship with Doc.

"He certainly had a huge influence on me. I would credit Doc and my father for helping me to be a lot less materialistic than I might have been. That was a very impressive thing about him."

As Robin became an adult, they grew to be equals and close friends. They sometimes travelled together, including an epic road trip to Vancouver near the end of Doc's life. After various jobs, including time with Customs and Excise Canada, the "dim-witted kid" went on to law school and became a Crown Prosecutor in Lethbridge with a wife and two children.

"Doc was probably the most remarkable and unique individual that I've ever encountered," Robin says, in summing up his friend. "I'm so fortunate to have known him as well as I did."

# CHAPTER 16
## Road Trip

Doc looked tired. Twenty-two years of providing medical service (sometimes for months at a stretch) from 1969 onward as the town's only doctor, had worn him down. He was 53 years old and needed a break.

In July of 1973, nurse Coreen Thacker called Robin Dann in Regina, where he was working, and suggested that he take Doc on a holiday. Doc was always reminiscing about his hometown and Coreen thought a trip to Vancouver might be the pick-me-up he needed. Robin was keen to go on a road trip with his friend.

It wasn't that Doc never got out of town for an extended break, but it didn't happen often. In 1961, he escaped Bow Island for a few weeks to take some medical courses at the Cook County Graduate School of Medicine in Chicago. Doc sent his parents in Toronto a postcard with a black and white photo of the modern, medical school building.

"Am having a fine time in Chicago," he wrote. "At Duncan YMCA. I play basketball, swim, lift weights, ping pong, etc etc. Saw the Chicago White Sox play baseball today. School courses very good. Lots to see. Costs me only $1.50 a day at the YMCA. - Harley."

On the trip, he got mugged by four guys in a rough part of Chicago. As they surrounded him, Doc dropped his valuables on the ground. The muggers decided to search him, because he had so little cash, and grabbed his car keys. He convinced them to give the keys back, since his car was thousands of miles away in Alberta.

On the way home, Doc stopped in Toronto to visit his parents and family. They picked him up at the airport where he was wearing a grubby, 75-cent, second-hand raincoat he had bought to replace the coat the muggers stole. His brother-in-law, Dick Shiozaki, gave him one of his old raincoats.

In 1967, the lure of Montreal's Expo 67 attracted Doc, like millions of Canadians. He decided to drive across the country and see the world's fair celebrating Canada's centenary year.

He took the two-week long trip with Hugh and Anne Louis and their niece. The four of them drove to Montreal in Doc's new car. For the first time that anyone can recall, Doc got his Medicare billings organized and filed them for payment, giving him enough money to buy a beige, 1967 Olds Delta 88.

"It's the only new car Doc ever had," says Hugh.

They camped along the way. Anne did most of the driving and pitched the tent every evening, while Doc sat back and had a smoke. They saw the highlights of Expo, including the American pavilion—a massive geodesic dome that floated like a soap bubble above the rest of the fair. Inside, an Apollo spacecraft hung from the ceiling and the work of a young artist named Andy Warhol confused visitors. On the way home, Doc and the Louises stopped in Toronto to visit Doc's parents and family. It was the last time Doc's family saw him alive.

"His family treated us very well," says Hugh. "Their son had come home for a change."

By 1973, it had been seven years since Doc had had any extended break from his medical practice. Robin arrived, in his 1964 Chevy Bel Air, to pick up his friend. Doc brought along his doctor's bag, a small satchel for clothes, a big hammer, and some cash. Actually, a fair amount of cash.

"Doc brought $700 in a wad," says Robin. "He lifted up the floor mat in the front seat and stuck it underneath the mat, and then said, 'Remind me not to forget it'. Doc is one of the only people I know that you'd need to remind."

They hit the road and drove more than 700 kilometres the first day, making it as far as Greenwood, B.C.. Robin expected them to look for a motel room, but Doc would have none of that.

"I'm not paying $25 for a motel, so pull over," said Doc, as Robin stopped along the side of the road. "I think I better get in the back seat," Doc added, before pulling his baseball cap down over his eyes and bedding down for the night.

Late the next day, they arrived in Vancouver. Doc was driving and he was thirsty. They hit various seedy bars before, exhausted, they decided to crash for the night. Robin wanted to rent a hotel room, but Doc didn't want to waste money.

"Doc drove onto the beach at Kitsilano. I say, 'We can't sleep on the beach in a car' but Doc disagreed," says Robin.

It was now two days on the road without a bed or shower and the travellers were grungy and tired. They headed over to Simon Fraser University in nearby Burnaby to visit Dr. Sam Smith, the newly appointed Dean of Arts and Sciences. Robin knew the young academic from Sam's days as the President of the University of Lethbridge, which are described as the most radical and exuberant in the history of the small Alberta university. Sam's new secretary eyed the pair suspiciously and told them the new dean hadn't arrived to start work yet, but was expected soon.

While they waited, Doc suggested they sneak into one of the university dorms and grab a free shower. As they headed out of the dorm, Doc stopped at a telephone booth and paged through the phone book looking for some listing he couldn't find. Eager to move on, Doc ripped the phone book out of the booth and stuffed it, and the trailing chain, into his pants pocket.

They returned to the dean's office and found him in. Sam eyed Doc, who stood there with the phone book and chain hanging out of his front pocket. Sam burst out laughing and said, "I'd have given you a phone book." He invited the pair to stay at his new home and they bedded down on the floor amid the moving boxes. One day during their stay, Doc borrowed the car keys and disappeared, coming back three days later.

As Robin and Doc drove through the streets of Vancouver, he reminisced about friends and events in his younger life. He was a good storyteller. Their travels never took them through his old neighbourhood or past the Nikaido family's home on Robson Street.

On the way out of Vancouver for the return trip, they stopped at a little hole in the wall where Doc grabbed a bag of fresh seafood to go. He sat back and contentedly munched away in the passenger's seat for the next hour, all the way to Abbotsford, the salty tang of the sea hanging in the close air.

When they reached Calgary, they stayed with one of Robin's friends. They arrived during Stampede Week and Doc, who never seemed to need much sleep, wanted to head out on the town. Robin, 28 years younger, was tired and due back at work in Regina shortly. Again, Doc borrowed the car keys for the night. This time he returned two days later.

Doc and Robin were gone for 10 days and drove 2,250 kilometres on a madcap road trip across two provinces, on what would be Doc's last holiday, but never once rented a motel room.

"We had tons of money, but Doc always said, 'I'm not paying $25 to sleep' and so we never once stayed in a room," says Robin.

# CHAPTER 17
## Doc's Personal Life

For a man who could be outspoken and brusque, Harry Nikaido was at heart a sensitive man who never talked about his personal life with anyone, even closest friends.

"I think in spite of his rough and gruff manner, he was shy inside," says sister, Geri Shiozaki.

She doesn't remember Doc having a girlfriend, as a teenager in Vancouver, as a student at University of Toronto, or during his adult life. University of British Columbia school chum Yoshio Hyodo doesn't recall any girlfriends either.

"As far as I know he wasn't interested in girls … we never talked about girls," says Yoshio. "When we two got together, it was nothing but sports."

Friends in Bow Island don't remember Doc having any romantic attachments, although he did chum around with one of the hospital's earlier nurse matrons in what was, by all appearances, a platonic relationship.

"I think he lacked confidence with women," says Heather Thacker, adding that the pool of available women in the Bow Island area, especially as Doc got older, was very small.

Left unsaid was the challenge, for an aging Japanese-Canadian bachelor, of finding an interested partner in southern Alberta in the 1950s and 1960s, when mixed-race romances and marriages were few and far between, and the pool of unattached Japanese-Canadian women was small.

Robin Dann says that Doc was a heterosexual man who simply never showed any interest in having a permanent or domestic relationship with a woman.

"He liked women but couldn't afford to date," says Margaret Anderson. "I think he was meant to be a bachelor and a doctor. Doc Nikaido wouldn't want to give up his lifestyle and no woman would want to put up with that."

Doc was guarded when it came to talking about family, other than to occasionally voice pride in their professional and educational accomplishments and to vent anger about their horrible treatment during World War II.

In the early 1950s, his father, Yoshi, travelled to Alberta to help Doc set up practice, but after 24 years in Bow Island, Doc had slowly drifted out of regular contact with family in Ontario.

His oldest brother, Sadao, had married and become a photographer at Simpsons-Sears. Frank, who like his sister was kicked out of the University of British Columbia during the war, never went back to university. He married and took over the family's dry cleaning business in Toronto. Geri was a mother, homemaker, and volunteer with seniors at the Japanese Culture Centre and other school and community groups.

Yoshi died in October, 1962, of cardiac amyloidosis, a disorder caused by deposits of abnormal protein in the heart tissue. He took his last English lessons only a few months before he passed away.

Doc only visited Toronto a half dozen times during his years in Alberta, the last time in 1967 on a return trip from Montreal's Expo 67. Doc was said to be planning a trip east with a friend when he passed away in 1975.

Doc never wrote his family and rarely phoned. When he did call, he always asked, "Is anyone sick?"

"He never talked about himself," says Geri. "We didn't know anything about his life in Bow Island. He could've been married for all we knew."

Kimi Nikaido regularly sent care packages to her son. One time in the 1960s, Robin was at Doc's office when Doc reached into a mountain of papers and pulled out a package with a pair of tan casual pants inside. He turned the pockets inside out and showed Robin that his mother had stitched and reinforced the pockets.

"She knows I carry loose change and all sorts of things in my pockets and am likely to wear holes in them and won't bother to stitch them up," Doc said.

On New Year's and other special occasions, Doc would arrive at Alex and Judy Zhou's hotel café with food packages from Kimi, which he reheated in the restaurant's kitchen.

Margaret attributes Doc's gradual loss of close contact with his Toronto family to a combination of being tied down by a busy rural practice and not being able to afford the cost of travelling.

"He got into a rut in Bow Island, and it wasn't easy to leave town because of his patients."

The picture painted is of a hardworking bachelor, far from family, wedded to his work. It is easy to see it as a lonely life, especially in the early days when he knew no one. Female friends and patients see it that way.

"I think he was lonely sometimes," says Judy Zhou. "I think that's why he sat in the bar."

Maybe Doc's unannounced house calls for supper at friends and patients' homes were about more than enjoying a good meal or a comfortable couch to watch television. Perhaps it was a desire for domestic warmth and companionship too. Still, Robin doesn't see his friend as a lonely man.

"I think there would've been aspects of his life that were lonely, but I don't think he was lonely," says Robin. "He could go anywhere and was welcome anywhere. He didn't have the intimacy of a family but he, in a sense, had a big family. Overall, I don't think he was a lonely person."

# CHAPTER 18
## A Night At The Hospital

For Dr. Harry Nikaido, a night of working at the hospital was a night spent at home. When he wasn't at his office, he spent much of the day working, eating, reading, and watching TV at the hospital. It wasn't unusual for him to spend the night sleeping on his side, stretched out across three plastic chairs in the dining room.

Heather Thacker, who worked permanent and part-time nights as a nurse in the early 1970s, says Doc slept at the hospital about one-third of the time.

"Where else was he going to go?" asks Heather. "I think he liked to be around the staff … and he had his TV set up in the dining room and he'd sit and watch TV when he wasn't busy."

He wouldn't hesitate to wander into the kitchen and make himself something to eat or go downstairs and use the laundry room to wash his clothes.

The staff, particularly the nurses, became his extended family. From the first day he arrived, Doc's approach was different from other doctors who came and went. He treated the nurses as equals and valued their input. This was a wild departure in protocol for the early 1950s. Doctors regarded nurses as underlings and nurses were trained to treat doctors as though they were gods. Nurses were never to fraternize with doctors, let alone be their partners in medicine.

"There was none of this 'on a pedestal' stuff ," says Coreen Thacker, Heather Thacker's sister and fellow nurse, who (like her elder sister) married a local farmer with the same family name.

"In the city hospitals, you scraped and bowed and stood up and sat down for the doctors. Doc never thought we weren't equal. We were just a team."

Late at night, Doc sometimes headed into the hospital kitchen to whip up a meal for the two nurses on night shift. Steaks, stir fry, and even squid, but more often than not he made western-style Chinese food. It was good, although from time-to-time ashes from his cigarette fell into the food as he cooked.

He did the same for patients. Teenager Larry Jenkins was hospitalized and hated the bland food. A couple of times during his stay, Doc made Chinese food for Larry in the middle of the night and they sat up together and ate. When Don Fraser was in for a broken ankle, Doc stopped by for a midnight visit with freshly made tea.

If he wasn't making the nurses food, he saw to their various ailments, as many of them and their families were patients. One time, he even made a foray into dentistry. Nurse Mavis Weatherhead had a bad toothache. Doc promptly pulled the offending tooth, without anaesthetic, in the hospital kitchen.

Occasionally he tried his hand at chiropractic medicine. Former nurse Sheila Bjerkseth says he worked on her troubled back and got it straightened out.

When Doc was on duty the hospital sometimes doubled as a veterinary clinic, at least in the early years. A technician walked in to find a whining German shepherd with a broken leg stretched out on the x-ray table. Another time Doc dipped into the hospital's pharmacy supplies to administer some nearly expired anti-venom to a dog who had been bitten by a rattlesnake.

Doc's intervention saved Ron Hyland's children's black dog after he had been run over on the road and had his leg broken. Given the severity of the injury, Ron had planned to take the dog to the farm and shoot him. Doc saw the crying children and told the Hylands to bring it in for him to have a look.

"Damned if Doc didn't make a plaster of Paris cast and the dog never had a limp afterward," says Alan, Ron's oldest son.

The nurses looked after Doc like a brother, especially the older nurses. They cut and dyed his hair. Mended his clothes and shortened his pant legs. They knew he wore a 27-inch leg and a 46-inch waist. Sometimes they grabbed his clothes while he was in his scrubs and threw them in the washing machine downstairs.

"At Christmas, everyone bought him clothing," says Heather. "I think that's the only way he got clothes. He was like a kid at Christmas opening the presents."

While most people considered Doc's nights at the hospital a selfless act of dedication or the actions of a bachelor lonely for companionship, others viewed them negatively. They were a problem for fellow doctors, and by extension, for the hospital board, its chair Alfred Egan, and the hospital administrator. It came down to money.

"There was no malice in his intent … the hospital was his home and he wasn't staying overnight for the money … he was doing it for the patients," says John Nicolet, hospital administrator from 1972 to 1976.

"For the nursing staff, it was a great thing, because if there was an emergency, there was a physician there," says John. "I didn't mind him staying overnight, because the nursing staff were happy and we gave better service."

Coreen agrees: "The nurses liked him … because as a nurse he never left you in the lurch. Never, ever."

John understood that Doc also liked staying at the hospital because cook Edie Hall made him "all kinds of meals and so of course he was in paradise."

"But his staying overnight created havoc, because it took patients from other doctors," says John. "It was affecting their billings and he was affect-ing their pocketbooks."

John was under pressure from Alfred and the board to ensure Doc didn't stay at the hospital overnight. They were desperate to keep the other doctors in town happy, in order to ensure there were other GPs in the community besides Doc.

"I talked to Doc and said, 'Doc, I'm getting too much pressure; you gotta get out of here.' He'd get out for a month and … all of a sudden an emergency would happen and he'd stay overnight. It was a continuous battle, he'd be out for a month and then he'd sneak back in."

**Doc poses in a corridor of the Bow Island Hospital on the 10-speed bike he was given as a present at a special event held earlier that evening to honour his 23 years of service in the community. The photo was taken on March 2, 1973.**

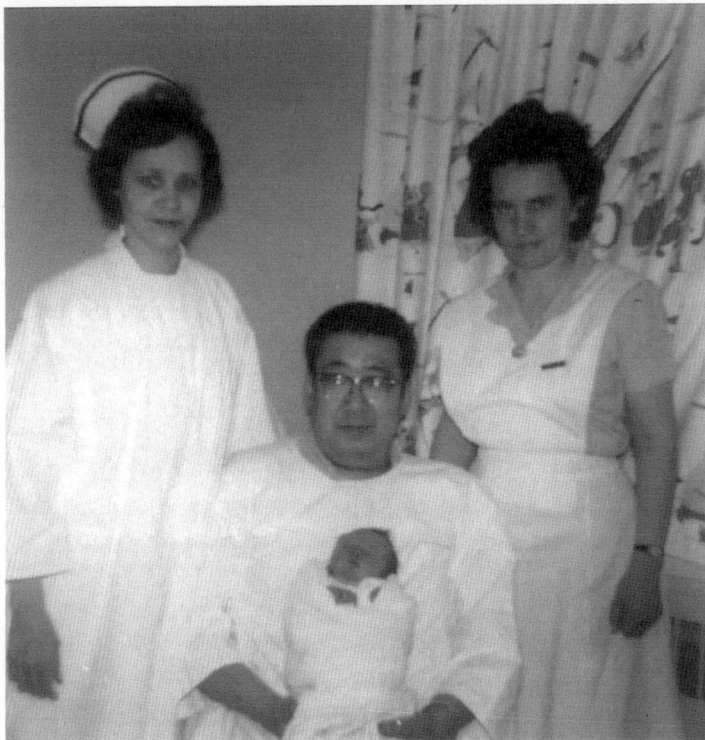

**Registered Nurse Maureen Corraini, left, and Nurses Aide Pearl Gatz, right, pose with Doc as he holds a baby believed to be Shannon Weatherhead in this photo from 1962 taken at the Bow Island Hospital.**

# CHAPTER 19
## The Hospital Crisis Of 1969

The year 1969 was momentous. Neil Armstrong and Apollo 11 landed on the moon in one giant leap for mankind. The Beatles decided to *Let It Be* and broke up. The super group Crosby, Stills, Nash, and Young performed together for the first time. It was the year of Woodstock, Vietnam War protests, and the election of President Richard M. Nixon. Canadians were still on a honeymoon with a young, bachelor prime minister named Pierre Elliott Trudeau.

It was momentous for Dr. Harry Nikaido too. After 18 years of faithfully serving Bow Island, his landlord evicted him from his office and he became embroiled in a hospital controversy that was the talk of the town. It culminated in a raucous public meeting attended by nearly 400 people.

The seed of the Hospital Crisis of 1969 was planted in 1968. The hospital board was looking to make changes at the Bow Island Hospital. It wanted doctors to perform more surgeries and to take on more complicated ones than the minor surgeries taking place. Doc was dead set against the proposal.

The board also wanted Doc and Dr. Stephen Carr, the town's other general practitioner, to move into a clinic together, something both opposed. The two physicians stayed clear of each other. They were like chalk and cheese. Dr. Carr was a middle-aged Englishman of patrician bearing. A formal, tie-wearing professional always addressed as "Doctor Carr." Doc was Doc, schlepping around sockless in untied shoes and dirty glasses. Not a formal bone in his body.

In 1968, the issue came to a head for Dr. Carr when the board suspended his hospital privileges, allegedly for not keeping his hospital patient files up to date. Dr. Carr said he never got a satisfactory explanation from the board for its decision. The board hid behind an arcane section of Alberta's Hospital Act, which said a board couldn't provide information about individual staff.

A frustrated Dr. Carr pulled out of Bow Island and set up practice in Medicine Hat. This left the town with only one doctor for the first time since 1953 and threatened the viability of the hospital. In a desperate bid to lure a new doctor to Bow Island, town council spent nearly $17,000 to build a doctor's residence near the baseball diamonds, complete with fridge and stove. It offered the house for rent at very reasonable terms to any new doctor. Council made no such offer to Doc who lived and slept either in his long-time office on the main street or at the hospital. Their efforts to woo someone proved successful when Dr. Ivan Kowalchuk moved to town in the summer of 1969.

The difference between council's efforts for a new doctor and its handling of Doc was further amplified when a councillor, Mildred Jensen, purchased the building containing Doc's office and began remodelling it without giving Doc any indication of his future prospects as a tenant. All this upset Doc, as did the lingering debate over Dr. Carr's departure, which saw the nurse matron and at least one other nurse leave the hospital.

"The trouble at the hospital was driving Doc around the bend," says Clara Fraser. "He was in a state."

At one point in Doc's discussions with Mildred, his new landlady, he became so paranoid that he bought a telephone tape recorder and began to record their conversations. He asked his part-time receptionist Linda Volk to transcribe the tapes.

His suspicions were well founded. After the remodelling job was complete, Mildred doubled Doc's rent and legally evicted him, forcing him out on the street. He was without a place to practise, or live, until a patient found him temporary space in a large, empty commercial building. She hung sheets to partition a space for Doc's "office."

As rumours swirled about town, Doc and his patients began to think that the hospital board and council were conspiring to try and drive him out of town. Doc's supporters talked about boycotting local merchants to put pressure on council. His friends organized a delegation, which met with council on December 8, 1969. They demanded to know why it had discriminated against Doc, offering housing incentives to any new doctor but nothing to Doc. Mayor Clarence Gatz insisted council was willing to help Doc too but had been rebuffed by Doc himself.

Doc's supporters formed a citizens' committee and organized a public meeting for December 15, 1969 to clear the air. They invited council and hospital board members to attend. They chose elementary school principal Ken Smith to chair the meeting held at the old community hall.

Nearly 400 people packed the hall, including reporters from the *Medicine Hat News* and *Taber Times*. Principal Smith, a Welsh orator with a deep voice, opened the meeting with an allegory, which compared rumour mongering with a cancerous growth. Smith noted that an infinitesimally-minute cancer cell eventually kills the organism in which it lives.

Alan Hyland, who would go on to serve as an Alberta Tory MLA for 18 years, remembers it as a wild meeting and one of the nastiest he ever attended in his early days in politics.

Initially council bore the brunt of the assembly's wrath as the hall's worn floorboards groaned under the shifting weight of the large audience. The focus shifted when, surprisingly, Dr. Stephen Carr rose to speak in support of Doc, with whom he had exchanged few civil words over their 14 years of working together. While they weren't friends, they respected each other professionally.

"Carr is a good doctor, but he gets some funny ideas about things," Doc once told Robin Dann.

In turn, Dr. Carr had described Doc as a "master doctor" in a conversation with Fred Mellen.

Dr. Carr laid the blame for the mess squarely at the feet of the hospital board. He said the board's suspension of his privileges related to their accusation that he was 500 records behind in his hospital files. He found this absurd, given that there were only 180 patient files at the hospital for the entire year and 100 of those were up to date.

"I am too old to enjoy being discarded like an old shoe at the whim of a secretive minority," Dr. Carr said, as he unbuttoned his tweed jacket and sat down.

Doc spoke and also blamed the hospital board, agreeing with Dr. Carr that it was inefficient. Doc said it made decisions without quorum and refused to give him, the town's only remaining doctor, any information about its rationale for making them. Doc disputed the board's accusations against Dr. Carr regarding patient files.

"I rarely have my case histories up to date and I wasn't suspended," said Doc. "The Bow Island Hospital Board must be investigated."

A member of the audience stood up and noted that if 25 per cent of the ratepayers of the district signed a petition requesting a public meeting, the hospital board was required to hold one. Following a tremendous round of applause, a petition asking the board to hold such a meeting was drawn up on the spot and promptly signed by 300 people.

The focus of the meeting moved on to Doc's lack of housing and office space. Doc described his unfair treatment at the hands of his building's new owner and introduced a series of affidavits and statements.

"The gist of his six-minute speech was that he had been mistreated," reporter Phil Johnson of the *Medicine Hat News* wrote in a story next day, headlined "Meeting Blasts Hospital Board". "Judging from the round of applause he received from the assembly, his dissertation was well taken."

Various speakers called on Mayor Gatz and council to build a suitable office and home for Doc. The mayor said he had no authority to take action without the approval of council and area ratepayers, who would have to foot the bill.

The tide turned when a speaker urged the audience to quit trying to force the mayor to do something beyond his power. Instead, those gathered decided to form a citizens' committee to help Doc find a living and office space. Eventually the group found a modest bungalow for Doc that was located between two double-wide trailers in the town's only trailer park. It was Doc's last office.

The meeting to rally support for Doc released a great pressure and slowly life in town, at the hospital, and for Harry Nikaido returned to normal. While friends agree it was a difficult and stressful year for Doc, it may also have been the making of him.

"It did hurt him, but there was a real rallying of most of the staff and the community around him," says Sheila Bjerkseth. "Afterward, he knew how much the community valued him."

"After that meeting, everything fell into place for him," says Clara.

"Looking back, it was the hospital crisis that was the turning point in his life," wrote Margaret Anderson years later. "To Dr. Nikaido, it must have been like the Japanese-Canadian evacuation all over again, only this time he won. He also won a lot of understanding from friends and patients. For once in his life, he felt truly accepted and confident in himself socially."

He got more invitations to dinner and to parties and went out more often. He joined the Legion and the Elks. Less than a year later, Doc ran for town council.

"In the end, Doc really gained by it, because he got so much support … and people didn't take him for granted any more," says Margaret.

# CHAPTER 20
## Doc Runs For Town Council

Twenty-eight years after Ottawa branded Harry Nikaido an enemy alien—making him an outsider in Canadian society (a role he chose to continue playing long after the war ended)—Doc reversed course and decided to become an insider. In a move that surprised friends, Doc ran for election to town council.

The man who had no time for authority, and even less for paying income tax, stepped forward to join a town council, which set and collected municipal property taxes, determined water rates, and created local bylaws. The rebel had decided to be become part of the establishment.

His decision came less than a year after the hospital controversy that almost forced him to leave town. Doc was emboldened by the public support he received during that tough year. He was curious to see if it would translate to the ballot box.

Margaret Anderson says Doc had always been interested in politics, but probably didn't think he had a chance of getting elected.

"After the hospital crisis, he felt he had a chance of winning and Doc liked to win," says Margaret, an outspoken commentator on community affairs and the first woman ever elected to the County of Forty Mile council.

Elections in rural Alberta in the 1970s were low-key, no-frill affairs. Campaigning was frowned upon. There were no election signs or speeches and few public debates. The local weekly newspaper ran a list of candidates standing for office and word got around the community. Municipal politicians were usually white, middle-aged men. One of five candidates in the contest to fill three vacancies, Doc won handily.

He served on a council, which included: Alan Hyland, who went on to become the area's Progressive Conservative MLA from 1975-1993; Phil Bryant, who later served as mayor of Drumheller, Alberta; and Mayor Fred Mellen, who was a councillor, mayor, and town development officer for many years.

Phil, a good friend of Doc's, thinks he entered politics because of his love for the community and because "he wanted the decisions of the day done right." He wanted the town properly run.

"The work was interesting to him and got him away from his medical thinking," says Phil.

Clearly there was something about serving on council that Doc enjoyed. Maybe it reflected a growing acceptance of his social responsibilities outside his professional life.

Council met every second Monday of the month at 7 p.m., in a boardroom at the town office that smelled of wax and floor polish. Sessions often lasted four or five hours. Doc's medical responsibilities kept him from attending some meetings, but he was there for big decisions on the major paving and sewer projects that dominated discussions of the time. With his keen mind and strong opinions, Doc made important contributions, one of which was to ensure any disagreements at council were left in council chambers after the decisions were made.

"I learned a lot from Doc, including not to hold a grudge," says former MLA and councillor Alan Hyland. "(Councillor) Roy Loney, Doc, and I had an agreement. We'd go to the hotel for a beer after council, no matter what the disagreement at council."

From time-to-time, Mayor Fred Mellen asked Doc to represent the town at various social functions. Inevitably, those in attendance were impressed.

"I always got feedback the next day of what a terrific job he had done," says Fred, a man with unmatched passion for his community. "He could speak, man."

During his time on council, Doc served on the town's police committee. Bow Island, like most rural Alberta communities, was serviced by a small RCMP detachment. The irony of Doc being on the police committee was not lost on the RCMP's Cpl. Barry Dilts.

"Doc hated cops, particularly the Mounted Police, because they were getting ready to move his family inland during the war," says Barry, who adds that, despite that impediment, the two become good friends during his three-year posting in Bow Island.

Phil and Fred say that Doc did a good job on council during his term. He enjoyed the challenges and change of pace from his normal work day so much that he re-offered in 1974. In that election, Doc was one of a handful of incumbents among the seven candidates running for six seats on council. Doc finished fifth and returned to council.

On Monday, November 3, 1975, Doc attended his last council session, a special meeting to hear appeals against two development permits the town had recently granted for a laundromat/dry cleaning business and for a self-serve gas station.

Doc would never enter the council chambers again. He died with 24 months remaining in his second term.

**Doc served on Bow Island Town Council from the Fall of 1970 until his death in 1975. He is pictured here with the 1974-75 version of council, from left: Roy Loney, H. Nielson, Alan Hyland, Walter Strom, Doc, Ralph Bateman, Town Secretary Vern Foss and Mayor Phil Bryant.**

# CHAPTER 21
## Doc's Death

By the fall of 1975 Dr. Harry Nikaido was exhausted. He had arthritis in his hands, high blood pressure, and an electrocardiogram that didn't look good. It wasn't surprising. He was overweight and hadn't gotten enough sleep for decades.

The tragedies and losses weighed heavily on him too, particularly the death on October 31, 1975 of Bertha Corraini, a 42-year-old widow and mother of four. She was not only a patient but a friend. Her death, and that of one of his young patients after a routine tonsillectomy done by a city doctor, were body blows to Doc. They aged him noticeably.

In the early evening on November 6, 1975, he walked into the Bow Island General Hospital as he had a thousand times before and headed into the doctor's room in the north wing, down the hall from the nurse's station. It had a bookshelf full of medical texts, a desk, and a single cot, on which (for some reason) Doc never slept. No one thought much about what Doc was up to until a nurse tried to use the hospital's one telephone line. It was busy. She tried the phone again and again, but it was in use from the doctor's room.

Heather Thacker was on duty as was Rosella Hadnagy. They walked down to the doctor's room to see why Doc was taking so long on the telephone. They knocked on the door, but there was no answer. They opened it and found Doc lying on the floor, eyes glazed, mouth foaming, one hand stretched out with a finger tapping the floor. The phone was off the hook.

It wasn't clear whether he was phoning someone or had knocked it off as he fell.

They asked Doc if he was okay, but he didn't reply. They quickly realized that he might have had a stroke. There were blood pressure pills in his pocket. There was no other doctor serving Bow Island, so they called for the volunteer ambulance to take him to the Medicine Hat Hospital. Before they left, Heather grabbed the EKG Doc had done one night after wincing in pain.

Heather accompanied Doc in the ambulance to Medicine Hat. She asked him to stick out his tongue, something she had heard him say to patients many times. He gamely tried but couldn't. Doc never regained consciousness, despite the hopes and prayers of hundreds of Bow Islanders.

Five days later, on November 11, as a chilly north wind blew along a light snowfall, Dr. Harry Nikaido passed away. At age 55, he died from the effects of a stroke resulting from a massive brain hemorrhage, and kidney failure. Patients, friends, and hospital staff were heartbroken. They had lost the town's lone doctor, a faithful medical practitioner, and a good friend.

"A friend that was an awful lot of fun," says Margaret Anderson. "I am sure many people miss him far more as a friend than they do as a doctor."

"He was one of the better friends I ever had," says Merle Nelson. "He'd give you the shirt off his back. I believed in him and so did my Mom. She thought the world of him."

"He was loyal to his friends and to the nurses for sure," says Mavis Weatherhead. "He was one of the great people of the world."

There was some guilt over Doc's passing too.

"We depended on him," says Mavis. "He looked after everyone but not himself."

"He was always on call for thee," says Coreen Thacker. "We used him up. I feel bad about that."

An editorial, which appeared in *The 40-Mile County Commentator* on January 30, 1974, more than one year before his death, had presciently lauded Doc for a record of unceasing service to the community.

"Occasionally we hear people grumbling and swearing when Dr. Harry Nikaido takes off a few hours for a curling game in the winter, or a couple of days for a golf tournament in the summer, but how many people stop to realize just how many hours of the day and how many hours of the week the friendly 'Doc' is on call?" the editorial asked.

"Simple mathematics tell us that there are 168 hours in every week. If Doc Nikaido was on call for forty of those hours, you would expect that more than three times out of four he would be unavailable. But Doc's record is much better than that! He's usually within reach, whether it's 2:30 in the afternoon or 2:30 in the morning, but being human, he needs an occasional moment to call his own.

"On numerous occasions, it seems, we have discovered that Doc Nikaido happened to be in the right place at the right time when an emergency occurred. One such occasion was last Sunday, when a little child was brought to the hospital with convulsions. Doc Nikaido wasn't curling. He was available to render help, and what a tremendous sense of relief it must have been for those anxious parents to see him there so soon.

"As we see it, it's good to give credit where credit is due. Bouquets to Doc Nikaido for many years of faithful service. He isn't everybody's idol. That's because he's human, and he needs an occasional curling game to keep him that way."

Robin Dann says all the years of medical service eventually wore his friend out.

"I think the 24/7 nature of his medical practice contributed to his early death. Toward the end, he knew his blood pressure was skyrocketing. He told me that he had an appointment with a specialist in Medicine Hat about it."

Days after Doc's passing, Margaret drove by the Myrtle Hotel and saw the bicycle given to him on his Recognition Night leaning forlornly against the hotel where Doc had left it.

"It was sad to see the bike there and no Doc to ever use it again."

# CHAPTER 22
## The Funeral

Tears streamed down trumpeter Bill Noviski's cheeks as he played *The Holy City* before a hushed crowd of more than 200 people crammed into Bow Island's St. Andrew's Church.

"It is with a tremendous sense of loss, both as individuals and as a community, that we gather in this place once again, to pay tribute to one of our citizens," said Reverend Oliver Hodge, the United Church Minister and publisher of *The 40-Mile County Commentator,* as he began the eulogy for Dr. Harry Nikaido.

"Many of you that are here today will know Doc Nikaido much better than I do, but in the four and a half years that we have been in this community, I have come to know him as a man of great compassion, and great knowledge. As I suggested to his brothers, Frank and Sadao, and his sister, Geri, he was like 'a diamond in the rough', lacking perhaps in a little of the polish and shine usually associated with his profession, but having many of the characteristics of a rare jewel."

Hugh Louis, sitting in the pews, nodded in agreement at the analogy, as did Doc's siblings. They were there without Doc's mother, Kimi, who at age 80, was too unwell to travel from Toronto.

"Doc will be greatly missed, both as a friend and as a family doctor; and the number of people here today testifies to the esteem in which he was held."

Oliver went on to paint a picture of a Doc the community knew so well, warts and all.

"Most of us realize that Doc was his own worst enemy. He would tell his patients and friends to lose weight, but if any of them dared to point out that he, too, had a bay window, he would probably pat it and say, 'that's all muscle.'"

*The New Canadian*, the Vancouver newspaper of record for Japanese-Canadians, which in the 1930s had toasted the athletic prowess of Har Nikaido, printed the eulogy on the front page of its January 6, 1976 edition, under the headline "Tribute to Nisei 'Doc' of Alberta Town."

Bill Noviski and piano accompanist Marguerite Nering played *In the Garden* for the recessional as Doc's casket was carried down the aisle by six pallbearers, including Alex Zhou, Don Fraser, and Robin Dann. Thirty nurses and staff, as well as Legion and Elks members, formed an honour guard as the casket left the church.

At the reception, which followed the burial in Bow Island Cemetery, Doc's family learned a great deal they had never known about his life during his 24 years in Bow Island. People stepped forward to recount stories about Doc to Geri, Frank, Sadao, and their spouses and children.

A ten-year-old boy made a point of telling Geri a story about bringing his sick dog to see Doc. He said Doc took the time to gently tell him that the dog didn't have long to live.

The Nikaidos were deeply touched to learn so much about their brother and uncle. They had last seen Doc in 1967, on his way home from visiting Expo '67.

His mother, Kimi Nikaido, wrote a Card of Thanks published in *The 40-Mile County Commentator* after Doc's funeral to his friends and patients "for the affection and care that you have shown to our late son and brother these many years."

"For us it is a great honour that 'Doc' is to remain here among you, his true family."

A Bow Island family, which had laughed and cried with Doc, fed and clothed him, and grown old with him. Brother-in-law, Dick Shiozaki, echoes Kimi's theme: "He looked after the patients but maybe the patients looked after him too."

One sign of that care was the detailed darns on his clothes that Geri noticed as Doc's family and friends went through the personal effects in his office, which included unopened packages from his family.

They also found crumpled dollar bills behind an examining table, as well as bundles of uncashed cheques from patients worth thousands of dollars for medical services rendered. Fitting reminders left behind by a man to whom money meant little or nothing.

# EPILOGUE

**"A man is not dead while his name is still spoken."**
**-- English author Terry Pratchett.**

The name of Dr. Harry Nikaido lives on in Bow Island, 38 years after his death. A complex man remembered in so many ways. An eccentric, lone wolf. A keen intelligence. A great doctor and better friend. A compassionate man of fierce convictions.

"To have a person remembered so deeply still is really something after all these years," says former Bow Island mayor Fred Mellen. "Everybody has a story to tell about Dr. Nikaido."

After his death, friends and patients formed a committee to raise money for a memorial fund to honour Doc, the way communities remember their heroes and pioneers. More than 300 people from three provinces and two American states donated $7,000, including the Bow Island branch of the Royal Canadian Legion.

The committee erected a headstone over Doc's grave with one line, which reads: "Life's Work Well Done." He is buried in the Bow Island Cemetery, beside the golf course. He rests among patients and friends on a slight knoll where a constant breeze intermingles with the meadowlark's song.

On June 27, 1977, the expansion to the newly renovated Bow Island Hospital was named the Dr. H. Nikaido Memorial Garden and Nursing

Home, to commemorate Doc's contribution to the community. The plaque reads: "Doc did so much, for so many, for so little."

"People will never ever see anyone like him again," says Linda Volk. "There are country doctors, but country doctors were never like Doc. If someone was really sick, he knew it and he knew what to do."

As a doctor, he marched to his own drummer.

"He didn't give a rip about a lot of things you would have thought a doctor would care about," says Linda. "He just wanted to practise."

Remarkably, the Alberta Health Department and provincial medical officials seem to have left Dr. Harry Nikaido alone to carry on his unorthodox practice in his unique way in this quiet corner of southeastern Alberta.

Former Bow Island hospital administrator John Nicolet says he never got one question from provincial health officials about why he had a doctor working in his hospital who didn't file Medicare claims, even at times when he was the only doctor in town.

Retired Crown prosecutor Robin Dann says he doesn't think today's world would accommodate someone like Doc.

"I don't know if you could survive in a profession doing that any more."

In a November 28, 1975 letter to *The 40-Mile County Commentator*, Margaret Anderson summed up the riddle that was Doc this way: "A man who you might say gave his life to the community, a man who suffered bitterly over the injustices done to Japanese people and who suffered racial discrimination perhaps more than others because he was too sensitive to take things like this lightly.

"How Dr. Nikaido could have become the dedicated doctor that he was, for a society that had done this to him and his people, is impossible to understand. The fact that he did this with so little remuneration is still harder to understand."

Which leaves one to wonder whether Dr. Harry Nikaido's life would have turned out differently if the Canadian government hadn't acted so unjustly against its Japanese-Canadians citizens during World War II.

Would Doc have spent his medical career in small town Alberta as a general practitioner, living a bachelor's life of poverty or would he have become a celebrated medical specialist and professor like some of his medical school friends?

Coreen Thacker says that, when Doc passed away, a medical classmate from University of Toronto called. He said Doc was in the top of their class and could have been whatever he wanted to be in the medical field.

Geri Shiozaki believes that, in finding Bow Island, her brother found a perfect home.

"I don't know if Har would've worked out in a more civilized place."

Robin agrees.

"I think that regardless of his skill as a physician … it would've been difficult to practise medicine in an urban setting and live his bohemian lifestyle," says Robin. "I think the small town was the one place where he could live the lifestyle that he wanted to live … and be accepted for what he was."

Robin believes that once Doc got settled in Bow Island, its advantages became clear.

"He realized there was a lot of business, and guess what, I don't have to wear a suit and have a receptionist. Once he dropped his anchor in Bow Island, maybe he realized he could practise medicine there without the restrictions he'd have in a big place."

As for what Doc's life would have been like if Canada hadn't unjustly turned Japanese-Canadians out of B.C.'s Garden of Eden, Robin offers this:

"It's fair to say it would've been a different story, but Doc would still have been an eccentric and a maverick."

At his death, friends offered two opposing views as to what shaped his life. In his eulogy, Rev. Oliver Hodge suggested that Doc's vow of poverty and his disregard for recompense was driven by his resentment of a Canadian government, which had unjustly treated his family and other Japanese Canadians.

"Having seen his parents and friends literally uprooted from their familiar surroundings, it left him with a very cynical and suspicious attitude towards government, and a determination that they would never have the opportunity of taking very much away from him," Oliver said.

In a letter to the *The 40-Mile County Commentator* following Doc's funeral, his U of T medical school classmate and friend Dr. J.H. (John) Toogood offered another view. Toogood had gone on to a distinguished career as a respected allergy specialist at the Victoria Hospital's Allergy Clinic in London, Ontario and was a faculty member at the University of Western Ontario medical school.

"I presume to disagree with the preacher at Harry's funeral when he implied that he never billed his patients because of a cynical and suspicious attitude toward the government," says Dr. Toogood.

"That's exactly the reason that I would expect Harry to have given if asked, but that doesn't truly reflect the real man – only the hard shell that he developed in self-defence.

"The way I read it, Harry practised medicine for love and not for money. He needed the people of Bow Island as much as they needed him – and in his very perceptive and realistic way, he could see this more clearly than many of us can – and that the 'hassles' of billings and creditors in this situation would be not only irrelevant, but actually counter-productive, a substitution of the symbol for the thing which was of real value to him.

"During the past 30 years I have met a few doctors, scattered over two continents, who share Harry's highly non-materialistic attitudes towards the practice of medicine. But they are rare birds and when we see one, we should study and think about it, because it will be a long time before we see another."

Perhaps both a hatred of Ottawa and a desire to help his fellow man drove Doc, the two motivations ebbing and flowing, sometimes one dominant, sometimes the other. His life was also shaped by a desire for intellectual challenge, which he satisfied through the practice of medicine, and later, by engaging in municipal politics.

The federal government's actions during World War II profoundly scarred Harry Nikaido. The young Harry saw himself as a Canadian—not as a hyphenated Canadian and certainly not as the enemy alien that his government branded him and other Canadians of Japanese descent. After the war, Harry never felt fully accepted in society, except among friends and those on the margins of society.

No one will ever know what motivated Dr. Harry Nikaido. Everyone who knew him, however, would agree with the closing line of Oliver's eulogy: "Doc was an individualist if there ever was one; like many of today's generation, 'he did his own thing.' But he was accepted for what he was … and loved for who he was … and it is appropriate that we will remember him in this way."

The last words are Heather Thacker's, who along with her sister, Coreen, and the other nurses in Bow Island, were Doc's second family.

"He was an original. An absolute original."

# ACKNOWLEDGEMENTS

Writing a book is a solitary endeavour, but the journey is never completed alone. There are so many people to thank for their advice, support, and assistance along the way.

I want to begin by thanking Dr. Harry Nikaido's sister, Geri Shiozaki, and her husband, Dick, and their daughter, Karie Shiozaki, who took a telephone call from a stranger and responded so graciously.

Margaret Anderson, who many years ago began work on a book about Doc's life, was extraordinarily helpful, providing me with her draft, including interviews with some of Doc's friends who were no longer with us by the time I began my research. As Sir Isaac Newton said: "If I have seen further than others, it is by standing upon the shoulders of giants."

The nursing sisters Coreen and Heather Thacker (my former babysitters), and Gail McNeely, were among my first interviewees as they worked alongside Doc for many years. They indulged me time and again as I sought out more information.

A non-fiction book cannot be completed without the assistance of trained archivists, librarians and photographers. Thanks to: Kimberley Unrau and Candace Loder, assistant archivists at the Esplanade Arts and Heritage Centre; Harold Averill, assistant university archivist at the University of Toronto; Kelly Hamilton, judicial clerk at the Medicine Hat Provincial Court; and Bow Island Municipal Library manager the late Susan Andersen and her staff. Also thanks to Jamie Rieger, Tom Conquergood and Pat McCray for access to *The 40-Mile County Commentator* files and to Bow Island town manager Anna-Marie Bridge and her staff. Thanks to photographer Paul Darrow for taking my portrait for the book's cover.

A special thank you to the team at FriesenPress and to my account managers, Kate Juniper and Jessica Palmer, for the good work, sound advice and timely assistance in making this book a reality.

While writing can be a lonely craft, it is less so with the support of a writer's circle for feedback on your work. I was blessed to have the careful eyes of Judith Scrimger, Val Spencer, Jodi Reid, Susan Drain, Sheila Morrison, and Rosemary Drisdelle to help guide me.

Robin Dann and Fred Mellen, two men with a passion for their home town, its history, and the role Dr. Harry Nikaido played in both, were instrumental in helping me complete this book. I can never repay their assistance, kindness and advice.

This book has been a labour of love, and so the last person I must acknowledge is the first person in my life—my wife, Karen Shewbridge. A card she once gave me has a quote from the Italian poet Arrigio Boito, which sums up our life together:

*When I saw you*

*I fell in love*

*And you smiled because you knew*

# SOURCES

## INTERVIEWS

The following people kindly agreed to be interviewed, some a number of times: Gerri, Karie and Dick Shiozaki; Nancy Shiozaki; Fred Mellen; Heather and Coreen Thacker; Gail and Blair McNeely; Don and Clara Fraser; Merle and Ella Nelson; Robin Dann; Margaret Anderson; Mavis and Larry Weatherhead; Morley Henningsgard; Karren Graham.

Linda Volk; Janice Goodfellow; Beverley Walker; George and Violet Lee; Alex and Judy Zhou;Hugh Louis; Wayne Barnes; Dr. Ernest Mastromatteo; Barry Dilts; Dixie Johnson; Sheila Bjerkseth; Phil Bryant; Carolyn Janzen; Rosella Hagnagy; Doris Campbell; John Nicolet; Yoshio Hyodo; Alan Hyland; Dalyce Bergen; Norm Noviski; George Thacker.

## BOOKS

Alberta History Along the Highway, by Ted Stone, Red Deer College Press, 2002

All Hell for a Basement, by Ed Gould, City of Medicine Hat, 1981

Down Memory Lane, Fred Mellen, 2012.

Monogatari: Tales of Powell Street (1920-1941); National Nikkei Museum, 2011

Mutual Hostages: Canadians and Japanese during the Second World War, Patricia E. Roy, J.L. Granatstein, Masako Iino and Hiroko Takamura, University of Toronto Press, 1990

Nishiki: Nikkei Tapestry: A History of Southern Alberta Japanese Canadians, published by the Lethbridge and District Japanese Canadian Association, 2001

Righting Canada's Wrongs: Japanese Canadian Internment in the Second World War by Pamela Hickman and Masako Fukawa, Formac Lorimer Books, 2012

Sage Brush to Pivots: A History of Bow Island and Area, Bow Island Historical Book Group, 2004

Silver Sage: Bow Island 1900 to 1920, Bow Island Lions Club, 1971

Southern Alberta: A Regional Perspective, edited by Dr. F. Jankunis, University of Lethbridge, 1972

The Battle of Belly River, compiled by Alexander Johnston, Lethbridge Branch of the History Society of Alberta, 1966.

The Great Adventure: How the Mounties Conquered the West, David Cruise and Alison Griffiths, Penguin Books, 1996

The Encyclopedia of Canada's Peoples, University of Toronto Press, 1999

The Japanese in Canada by W. Peter Gard, Ottawa, 1983

The Politics of Racism by Ann Gomer Sunahara, Publisher Ann Gomer Sunahara, 2000

Wolf Willow: A History, A Story, and a Memory of the Last Plains Frontier, by Wallace Stegner, 1990, Penguin Books

## NEWSPAPERS

The New Canadian – Nov. 8, 1940 – "Maikawas Meet M & N"

The New Canadian – May 14, 1941 – "Ten Niseis to Receive Degrees in Annual UBC Graduation"

The New Canadian, July 12, 1947 – "Nine Graduate in Class of '47 from Toronto"

The Varsity – 1944 – "Varsity Lacrosse Whiz is All-Round Student Athlete"

The Graphic, (Bow Island) – Feb. 26 1959 - An 8-page special section on the opening of the new hospital

The Medicine Hat News – Dec. 16, 1969 - "Meeting Blasts Hospital Board"

The 40-Mile County Commentator – July 11, 1973 – "Court News"

The 40-Mile County Commentator - January 30, 1974 - "Credit Where Credit is Due" (editorial)

The 40-Mile County Commentator – Oct. 23, 1974 – "Six Elections Held in County and Area"

The 40-Mile County Commentator –Nov. 19, 1975 – "Bow Island Town Council Holds Special Meeting"

The 40-Mile County Commentator – Nov. 19, 1975 "Large Crowd Attends Funeral For Dr. Harry Nikaido, 55" and "Editorial or Sermon?"

The New Canadian – Jan. 6, 1976 – "Tribute to Nisei "Doc" Of Alberta Town"

The Ubyssey – May 30, 2012 – "Seventy years later, interned Japanese-Canadian students get honorary degrees"

## WEBSITES

SEDAI: The Japanese Canadian Legacy Project

cIRcle – A University of British Columbia digital repository for published and unpublished material – An interview with Geri Shiozaki, a UBC Japanese-Canadian student of 1942 and her husband, F. Richard (Dick) Shiozaki